Dr. Liew Voon Kiong

Visual Basic
2010

**Made
Easy**

Disclaimer

Visual Basic 2010 ® Made Easy- A complete tutorial for beginners is an independent publication and is not affiliated with, nor has it been authorized, sponsored, or otherwise approved by Microsoft Corporation.

Trademarks

Microsoft, Visual Basic, Excel and Windows are either registered trademarks or trademarks of Microsoft Corporation in the United States and/or other countries. All other trademarks belong to their respective owners.

Liability

The purpose of this book is to provide basic guides for people interested in Visual Basic 2010 programming. Although every effort and care has been taken to make the information as accurate as possible, the author shall not be liable for any error, harm or damage arising from using the instructions given in this book.

ISBN-13: 978-1467975193
ISBN-10: 1467975192
Printed in the United States of America

Acknowledgement

I would like to express my sincere thanks to many people who have made their contributions in one way or another to the successful publication of this book. My special thanks go to my children Xiang, Yi and Xun who have contributed their ideas and edited this book. I would also like to appreciate the support provided by my beloved wife Kim Huang and my youngest daughter Yuan. I would also like to thank the million of guests who have visited my **Visual Basic Tutorial** website at www.vbtutor.net for their support and encouragement.

About the Author

Dr. Liew Voon Kiong holds a bachelor degree in Mathematics, a master degree in Management and a doctoral degree in Business Administration. He has been involved in programming for more than 15 years. He created the popular online Visual Basic Tutorial at www.vbtutor.net in 1996 and since then the web site has attracted millions of visitors .It is one of the top ranked **Visual Basic** websites in major search engines including Google. In order to provide more support for the Visual Basic hobbyists, he has written this book based on the Visual Basic 2010 tutorial. He is also the author of **Visual Basic 6 Made Easy** and **Excel VBA Made Easy.**

TABLE OF CONTENTS

Chapter 1

Introduction to Visual Basic 2010

❖ A brief description of Visual Basic 2010

❖ Getting to know the Visual Basic 2010 Integrated Development Environment

1.1 A brief Description of Visual Basic 2010

Visual Basic 2010 is the latest version of Visual Basic launched by Microsoft in 2010. It is almost similar to Visual Basic 2008 but it has added many new features. Visual Basic has gone through many phases of development since the days of BASIC that was built for DOS. BASIC stands for **B**eginners' **A**ll-purpose **S**ymbolic **I**nstruction **C**ode. The program code in Visual Basic resembles the English language. Different software companies had produced many different versions of BASIC for DOS, such as Microsoft QBASIC, QUICKBASIC, GWBASIC, and IBM BASICA and more. Then, Microsoft launched the first graphical BASIC, Visual Basic Version 1 in 1991. It is GUI based and especially developed for MS window. Since then Microsoft slowly phased out the DOS versions of BASIC and completely replaced them by Visual Basic.

Visual Basic was initially a functional or procedural programming language until the popular Visual Basic 6. Then, Microsoft transformed Visual Basic into a more powerful object oriented programming language by launching Visual Basic.Net, Visual Basic 2005, Visual Basic 2008 and the latest Visual Basic 2010. Visual Basic 2010 is a full-fledged Object-Oriented Programming (OOP) Language; it has caught up with other OOP languages such as C++, Java, C# and others. However, you do not have to know OOP to learn VB2010. In fact, if you are familiar with Visual Basic 6, you can learn VB2010 effortlessly because the syntax and interface are almost similar. Visual Basic 2010 Express Edition is available for free download from the Microsoft site as shown below:
http://www.microsoft.com/visualstudio/en-us/products/2010-editions/express

1.2 Navigating the Visual Basic 2010 Integrated Development Environment

1.2.1 The Start Page

When you launch Visual Basic 2010 Express, you can see the start page of the Integrated Development Environment, as shown in Figure 1.1.

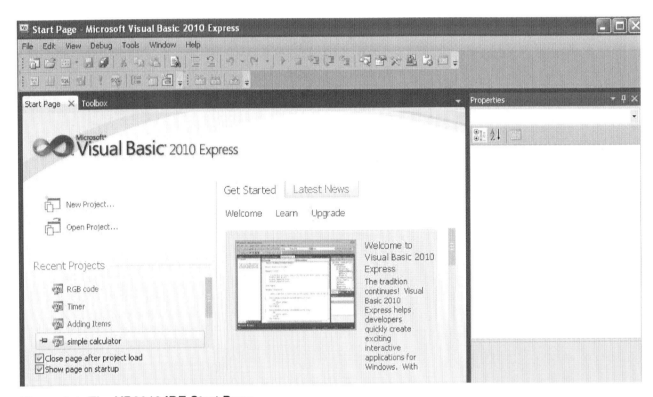

Figure 1.1: The VB2010 IDE Start Page

The IDE consists of a few panes, namely:

- The Recent Projects Pane- it shows the list of projects that you have created recently.
- The Get Started Pane- It provides some helpful tips so that you can quickly develop your new application.
- The Latest News pane- It provides latest online news about Visual Basic 2010 Express. It will announce new releases and updates.

Besides that, it also shows two icons, New Project and Open Project.

1.2.2 The New Project Dialog

When you click on the **New Project** icon, the Visual Basic 2010 New Project dialog will appear, as shown in Figure 1.2

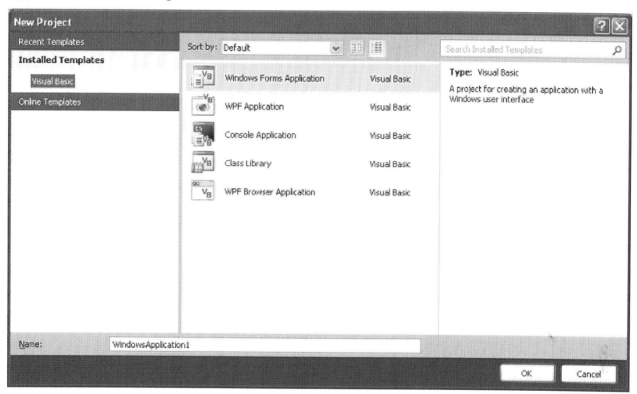

Figure 1.2: VB2010 New Project Dialog

The dialog box offers you five types of projects that you can create. They are Windows Form Application, WPF Application, Console Application, Class Library and WPF Browser Application. As we are going to create a standard Windows application, we will select Windows Forms Application. At the bottom of this dialog box, you can change the default project name **WindowsApplication1** to some other name you like, for example, **MyFirstApplication**. After you have renamed the project, click OK to go into the Designer interface.

1.2.3 The Designer Interface

The VB2010 IDE Designer interface is shown in Figure 1.3. The Designer consists of the **Menu bar**, the **Toolbars**, an empty **Form**, the **Solution Explorer** and the **Properties Window**. The VB2010 Designer environment that appears on your PC or laptop might not be the same here, depending how you customize it. You can customize your interface by dragging the windows and dock them or let them float. You can also hide them. To dock a window, you drag its title bar and drag it to the side, top or bottom of the workspace or another window. In Figure 1.3, we have dragged the Solution Explorer and the Properties Window to the side and docked them. You can also resize the docked window by dragging the side of the window. To free up and float the docked window, you just drag its title bar and move it away from the edge of the workspace. If you do not see a particular window such as the properties window, you can click on the View menu and click the name of the window, that particular window will appear.

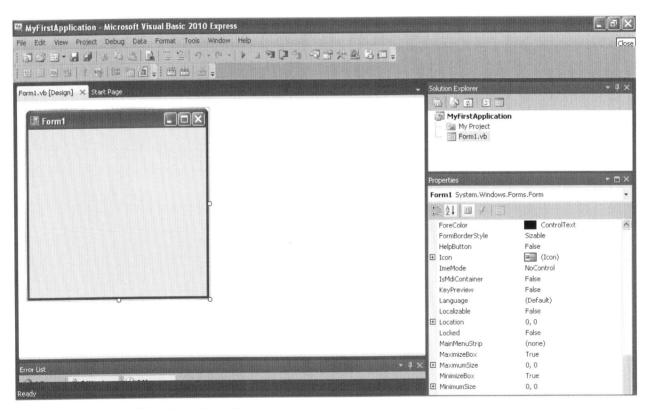

Figure 1.3: VB2010 IDE with A New Form

> **Form**-The Form is the first place to build your application. It is the place to design the user interface.
> **Solution Explorer** -The solution explorer displays a list of projects, files and other components that you can easily browse and access. For example, it displays My Project and Form1.vb in Figure 1.3
> **Properties Window-** This is the place to set the properties of the objects in your application. The objects include the default form and the controls you place in the form. We will learn more about setting properties later.

1.3 Understanding the Concept of Object Oriented Programming

The main different between VB2010 and Visual Basic 6 is that is it is a full Object Oriented Programming Language while VB6 may have OOP capabilities, it is not fully object oriented. In order to qualify as a fully object oriented programming language, it must have three core technologies namely **encapsulation, inheritance** and **polymorphism**. Read more about the three terms in the box below:

Encapsulation refers to the creation of self-contained modules that bind processing functions to the data. These user-defined data types are called classes. Each class contains data as well as a set of methods, which manipulate the data. The data components of a class are called instance variables and one instance of a class is an object. For example, in a library system, a class could be member, and John and Sharon could be two instances (two objects) of the library class.

Inheritance

Classes are created according to hierarchies, and inheritance allows the structure and methods in one class to be passed down the hierarchy. That means less programming is required when adding functions to complex systems. If a step is added at the bottom of a hierarchy, then only the processing and data associated with that unique step needs to be added. Everything else about that step is inherited. The ability to reuse existing objects is a major advantage of object technology.

> **Polymorphism**
>
> Object-oriented programming allows procedures about objects to be created whose exact type is not known until runtime. For example, a screen cursor may change its shape from an arrow to a line depending on the program mode. The routine to move the cursor on screen in response to mouse movement would be written for "cursor," and polymorphism allows that cursor to take on whatever shape is required at run time. It also allows new shapes to be integrated easily.

VB2010 is a fully Object Oriented Programming Language, just like other OOP such as C++ and Java. It is different from the earlier versions of VB because it focuses more on the data itself while the previous versions focus more on the actions. Previous versions of VB are **procedural** or **functional** programming language. Some other procedural programming languages are C, Pascal and Fortran.

VB2010 allows users to write programs that break down into modules. These modules represent the real-world objects; we also call them classes or types. An object can be created out of a class , it is an instance of the class. A class can also comprise subclass. For example, apple tree is a subclass of the plant class and the apple in your backyard is an instance of the apple tree class. Another example is student class is a subclass of the population class while a student with the name John is an instance of the student class. A class consists of data members as well as methods. In VB2010, the program structure to define a population class can be written as follows:

```
Public Class Population
'Data Members
Private Name As String
Private Birthdate As String
Private Gender As String
Private Age As Integer
'Methods
Overridable Sub ShowInfo( )
```

```
MessageBox.Show(Name)

MessageBox.Show(Birthdate)

MessageBox.Show(Gender)

MessageBox.Show(Age)

End Sub

End Class
```

After you have created the population class, you can create a subclass that inherits the attributes or data from the population class. For example, you can create a student class that is a subclass of the population class. Under the student class, you do not have to define any data fields that were already defined under the population class; you only have to define the data fields that are different from an instance of the population class. For example, you may want to include StudentID and Address in the student class. The program code for the StudentClass is as follows:

```
Public Class Student

Inherits Population

Public StudentID as String

Public Address As String

Overrides  Sub ShowInfo( )

MessageBox.Show(Name)

MessageBox.Show(StudentID)

MessageBox.Show(Birthdate)

MessageBox.Show(Gender)

MessageBox.Show(Age)

MessageBox.Show(Address)

End Sub
```

Summary

➢ In section 1.1, you learned about the evolution of Visual Basic.

➢ In section 1.2, you learned how to launch the start page, the new project dialog and the designer interface. In addition, you have learned that the designer interface comprises the Form, the Solution Explorer and the Properties window.

➢ You have also learned some basic concepts of object oriented programming, which comprises encapsulation, polymorphism and inheritance.

Chapter 2

Designing the Interface

- ❖ Learn How to Design the Interface
- ❖ Adding Controls
- ❖ Setting Control Properties

2.1 Adding Controls to the Form

The first step in creating a new VB2010 project is to design the interface of the application. You design an interface by adding controls to the form and then set their properties. You can add controls from the Toolbox. To see the Toolbox window, you can use the short-cut keys Ctrl+Alt+X or click on the Toolbox icon on the toolbar on top of the designer environment. The Toolbox consists of many useful controls such as Button, TextBox, Label, ComboBox, CheckBox and more, as shown in Figure 2.1

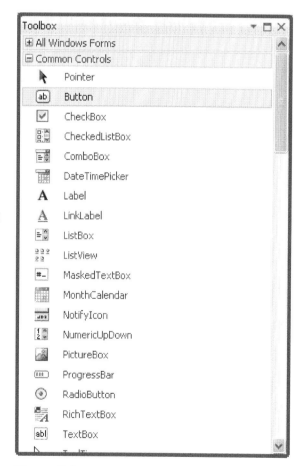

Figure 2.1

The Visual Basic 2010 Control Toolbox consists of all the controls essential for developing a VISUAL BASIC 2010 application. Controls in VB2010 are useful tools that can perform various tasks. We categorized into Common Controls, Containers, Menus, Toolbars, Data, Components, Printings and Dialogs. Now, we will focus on the common controls. Some of the most used common controls are Button, Label, ComboBox, ListBox, PictureBox, TextBox and more. To add a control to the form, just drag the particular control and drop it into the form. After putting it into the form, you can change its size and position easily. You can add as many controls as you want, but avoid crowding the form.

2.2 Setting the Control Properties Using Properties Window

To customize the interface to the users, you need to set the properties of the controls, from the form itself to the controls you add to the form. You can set the properties of the controls in the properties window at design time or by using the code. We shall learn how to set the control properties using the properties window first.

To set the properties of an object, right click on the object and choose properties in the dialog that appears to view the properties window. In the properties window, you can change the values of the properties that appear in a dropdown list, as shown in Figure 2.2. It is a typical Properties window for a form. The default text of the Text property is Form1, its default name is also Form1. You can change the title of the text to whatever title you like by editing the text.

The properties of the object appear in a list in the left column while the items listed in the right column represent the states or values of the properties. You can set the properties by highlighting the items in the right column then change them by typing or by selecting options. For example, to change the form's title to any name that you like, simple click in the box on the right of the Text property and type in the new name. In the properties window, the item appears at the top part is the currently selected object.

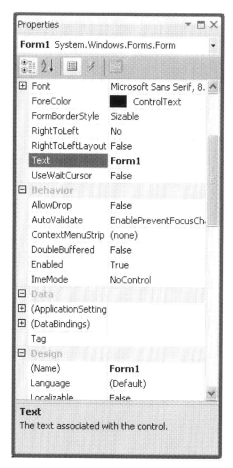

Figure 2.2: The Properties Window

Example 2.1: Creating a Simple Program that display a welcoming message

In this example, we will create a simple program that will display a welcome message when you load the form. First, change the properties of the form as follows:

Property	Value
Name	WelcomeMsgFrm
BackColor	Pink(background of the form)
Font	Microsoft Sans Serif Size 10 and Bold
ForeColor	White (The color of text on title bar)
Text	Visual Basic 2010 (Text on title bar)

Table 2.1: Properties of the Form

Next, insert a label into the form and set its properties as follows:

Property	Value
Autosize	False
Name	MsgLbl
BackColor	Purple
BorderStyle	FixedSingle
Font	Microsoft Sans Serif Size 10 and Bold
ForeColor	White
Text	Blank it

Table 2.2: Properties of the Label

Next, click on the Form and enter the following code:

```
Private Sub WelcomeMsgFrm_Load(ByVal sender As System.Object, ByVal e As System.EventArgs) Handles MyBase.Load

    MsgLbl.Text = "Welcome to VB2010 Programming"

End Sub
```

Run the program and the message is displayed on the label, as shown in Figure 2.3

Figure 2.3

2.3 Setting Control Properties using Code

You can also change the properties of the object using code. The syntax to manipulate the properties of an object is

Object.property=property_Value

For example,

TextBox1.Text="Welcome to VB2010"
TextBox2.Text=100

The above code sets the text property of TextBox1 to display the text "Welcome to VB2010" and set the value of TextBox2 to 100.

Other properties you can change to give special effects at runtime are color, shape, animation effect and so on. For example, the following code will change the form color to yellow every time the form is loaded. VB2010 uses RGB (Red, Green, Blue) to determine the colors. The RGB code for yellow is 255, 255, 0. Me in the code refers to the current form and Backcolor is the property of the form's background color. The formula to assign the RGB color to the form is Color.FormArbg(RGB code). Now, click on the form to go into the code window. Next, enter the following code between the opening statement Private Sub and the closing statement End Sub, as shown below. You don't have to worry about the code and the code structure yet; we will explain that in chapter 3.

```
Public Class Form1
Private Sub Form1_Load(ByVal sender As System.Object, ByVal e As
System.EventArgs) Handles MyBase.Load
    Me.BackColor = Color.FromArgb(255, 255, 0)
End Sub
End Class
```

Now Press F5 and you will see a form appear with a yellow background, as shown in Figure 2.4

14

You may also use the following procedure to produce the same effect.

```
Private Sub Form1_Load(ByVal sender As System.Object, ByVal e As
System.EventArgs) Handles MyBase.Load
    Me.BackColor = Color.Yellow
End Sub
```

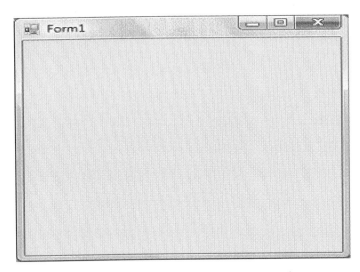

Figure 2.4: The form with yellow background

Here are some of the common colors and the corresponding RGB codes. You can always experiment with other combinations, but remember the maximum number for each color is 255 and the minimum number is 0. The table below shows some of the common colors with their corresponding codes.

Color	RGB Code	Color	RGB Code	Color	RGB Code
Red	255, 0, 0	Yellow	255, 255, 0	Orange	255, 165, 0
Green	0, 255, 0	Cyan	0, 255, 255	Black	0, 0, 0
Blue	0, 0, 255	Magenta	255, 0, 255	White	255, 255, 255

Table 2.5: Common colors and their corresponding RGB codes

The following is a program that allows the user to enter the RGB code into three different Textboxes and when he or she clicks the Display Color button, the background color of the form changes according to the RGB code.

The code

```
Private Sub Button1_Click(ByVal sender As System.Object, ByVal e As
System.EventArgs) Handles Button1.Click
        Dim rgb1, rgb2, rgb3 As Integer
        rgb1 = TextBox1.Text
        rgb2 = TextBox2.Text
        rgb3 = TextBox3.Text
        Me.BackColor = Color.FromArgb(rgb1, rgb2, rgb3)
End Sub
```

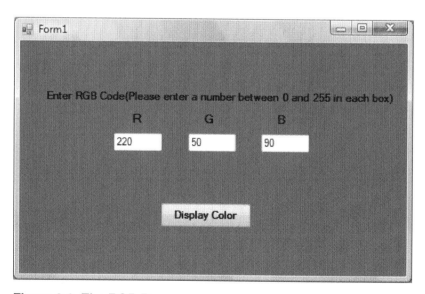

Figure 2.6: The RGB Program

Summary

➢ In section 2.1, you learned how to add controls to the form from the Toolbox.

➢ In section 2.2, you learned how to set the properties of the controls using the properties window.

➢ In section 2.3, you learned how to set the properties of the controls using code. For example, you learned how to set foreground and background colors using RGB code.

Chapter 3

Writing the Code

❖ Learn how to write Visual Basic 2010 Code

In the previous chapter, you have learned to design an interface, adding controls and setting control properties. You have also learned how to write some simple code without understanding the concepts behind. In this chapter, you will learn some basic concepts about VB2010 programming and the techniques in writing code .I will keep the theories short so that it would not be too taxing for beginners.

3.1 Understanding Event Driven Programming

VB2010 is an object oriented and event driven programming language. In fact, all windows applications are event driven. Event driven means the user decides what to do with the program, whether he or she wants to click the command button, enter text in a text box, or close the application and more. An event is related to an object, it is an incident that happens to the object due to the action of the user, such as a click or pressing a key on the keyboard. A class contains events as it creates instant of a class or an object. When we start a windows application in VB2010 in previous chapters, we will see a default form with the Form1 appears in the IDE. Form1 is the Form1 Class that inherits from the Form class System.Windows.Forms.Form, as shown in Figure 3.1

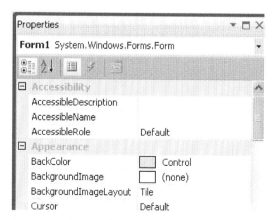

Figure 3.1: The Form1 Class

The other events associated with the Form1 class are click, DoubleClick, DragDrop, Enter and more, as shown in Figure 3.2 below (It appears when you click on the upper right pane of the code window)

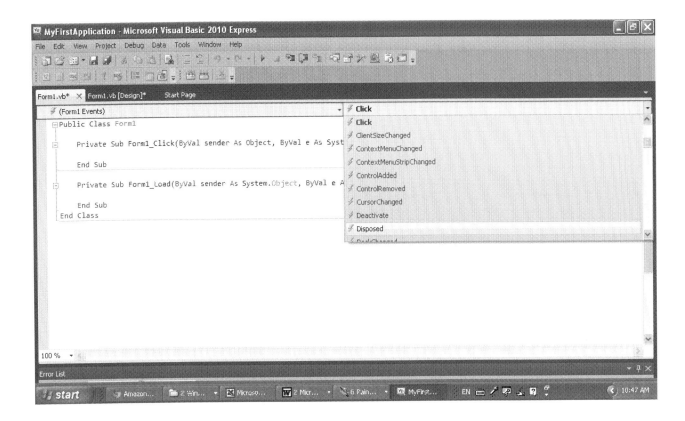

Figure 3.2: List of Events

3.2 Understanding the Code Structure of an Event Procedure

Now you are ready to write the code for the event procedure so that it will do something more than loading a blank form. The structure of the code takes the following form:

> Private Sub...
>
> Statements
>
> End Sub

You have to enter the code between Private Sub and End Sub.

Private Sub

Enter your code here

End Sub.

There are variations of the structure such as

i)   Public Sub

Enter your code here

End Sub.

ii)   Sub

Enter your code here

End Sub.

iii)   Function

Enter your code here

End Function

Let us enter the following code:

```
Private Sub Form1_Load(ByVal sender As System.Object, ByVal e As
System.EventArgs) Handles MyBase.Load

        Me.Text="My First VB2010 Program"

        Me.ForeColor = Color.Yellow

        Me.BackColor = Color.Blue


End Sub
```

When you press F5 to run the program, the output is shown in Figure 3.3 below:

Figure 3.3: The Output Window

The first line of the code will change the title of the form to "My First VB2010 Program" , the second line will change the foreground object to yellow(in this case, it is a label that you insert into the form and change its name to Foreground) and the last line changes the background to blue color. The equal sign in the code is to assign something to the object, like assigning yellow color to the foreground of the Form1 object (or an instance of Form1). **Me** is the name given to the Form1 class. We can also call those lines as Statements. Therefore, the actions of the program will depend on the statements entered by the programmer. Here is another example.

```
Private Sub Button1_Click_1(ByVal sender As System.Object, ByVal e As
System.EventArgs) Handles Button1.Click

        Dim name1, name2, name3 As String
        name1 = "John"
        name2 = "Chan"
        name3 = "Ali"
        MsgBox(" The names are " & name1 & " , " & name2 & " and " & name3)

End Sub
```

In this example, you insert one command button into the form and rename its caption as Show Hidden Names. The keyword Dim is to declare variables name1, name2 and name3 as string, which means they can only handle text. The function MsgBox is to display the names in a message box that are joined together by the "&" signs. The output is shown in Figure 3.4 below:

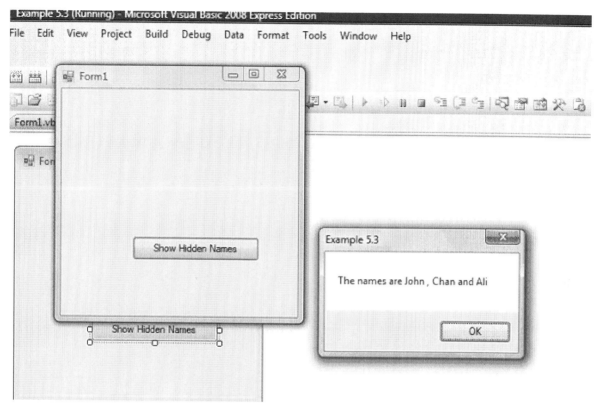

Figure 3.4: The Output Window for Displaying Names

3.3 Writing a Simple Multiplication Program

In this program, you insert two text boxes, three labels and one button. The text boxes are for the user to enter numbers, the label is to display the multiplication operator and the other label is to display the equal sign. The last label is to display the answer. The run time interface is shown in Figure 3.5

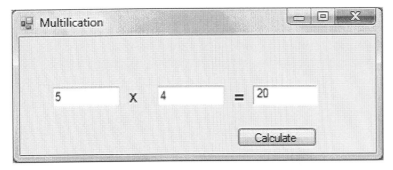

Figure 3.5: The Multiplication Program

The Code

Private Sub Button1_Click(ByVal sender As System.Object, ByVal e As System.EventArgs) Handles Button1.Click

```
    Dim num1, num2, product As Single
    num1 = TextBox1.Text
    num2 = TextBox2.Text
    product = num1 * num2
    Label3.Text = product
```

End Sub

3.4 Writing a Program that Add Items to a List Box

This program will add one item at a time to a list box as the user enters an item into the text box and click the Add button. In this program, you insert a TextBox and a ListBox into the Form. The function of the TextBox is to let the user enter an item one at a time and add it to the Listbox. The method to add an item to the ListBox is Add. The code is shown overleaf and the output interface is shown in Figure 3.6.

```
Private Sub Button1_Click(ByVal sender As System.Object, ByVal e As
System.EventArgs) Handles Button1.Click

        Dim item As String
        item = TextBox1.Text

        'To add items to a listbox
        ListBox1.Items.Add(item)

End Sub
```

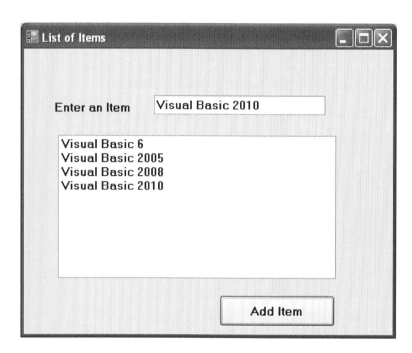

Figure 3.6: The Add Items Program

Summary

➢ In section 3.1, you learned the concept of event driven programming.

➢ In section 3.2, you learned how to write a simple code for an event procedure, including the usage of MsgBox().

➢ In section 3.3, you learned how to create a multiplication program.

➢ In section 3.4, you learned how to write code to add some items to a list box.

Chapter 4

Managing VB2010 Data

❖ Getting to know various data types in Visual Basic 2010

❖ Assigning values to the variables

❖ Getting to know various arithmetic operators in Visual Basic 2010

In our daily life we come across many types of data. For example, we need to handle data such as names, addresses, money, dates, stock quotes, statistics and more everyday. Similarly, in Visual Basic 2010, we have to deal with all sorts of data; some are numeric in natrure while some are in the form of text or other forms. VB2010 divides data into different types so that it is easier to manage when we need to write the code involving those data.

4.1 Visual Basic 2010 Data Types

Visual Basic classifies the information mentioned above into two major data types; namely the numeric data types and the non-numeric data types.

4.1.1 Numeric Data Types

Numeric data types are types of data that consist of numbers, which you can compute them mathematically with various standard operators such as add, minus, multiply, divide and so on. Examples of numeric data types are your examination marks, your height and your weight, the number of students in a class, share values, price of goods, monthly bills, fees and more. In Visual Basic 2010, we divide numeric data into seven types, depending on the range of values they can store. Calculations that only involve round figures or data that do not need precision can use Integer or Long integer in the computation. Programs that require high precision calculation need to use Single and Double decision data types, we also call them floating-point numbers. For currency calculation, you can use the currency data types. Lastly, if even more precision is requires which involve many decimal points, we can use the decimal data types. We summarized the data types in Table 4.1

Type	Storage	Range of Values
Byte	1 byte	0 to 255
Integer	2 bytes	-32,768 to 32,767
Long	4 bytes	-2,147,483,648 to 2,147,483,648
Single	4 bytes	-3.402823E+38 to -1.401298E-45 for negative values 1.401298E-45 to 3.402823E+38 for positive values.
Double	8 bytes	-1.79769313486232e+308 to -4.94065645841247E-324 for negative values 4.94065645841247E-324 to 1.79769313486232e+308 for positive values.
Currency	8 bytes	-922,337,203,685,477.5808 to 922,337,203,685,477.5807
Decimal	12 bytes	+/- 79,228,162,514,264,337,593,543,950,335 if no decimal is use +/- 7.9228162514264337593543950335 (28 decimal places).

Table 4.1: Numeric Data Types

4.1.2 Non-numeric Data Types

Nonnumeric data types are data that cannot be manipulated mathematically using standard arithmetic operators. The non-numeric data comprises text or string data types, the Date data types, the Boolean data types that store only two values (true or false), Object data type and Variant data type .We summarized them in Table 4.2

Data Type	Storage	Range
String(fixed length)	Length of string	1 to 65,400 characters
String(variable length)	Length + 10 bytes	0 to 2 billion characters
Date	8 bytes	January 1, 100 to December 31, 9999
Boolean	2 bytes	True or False
Object	4 bytes	Any embedded object
Variant(numeric)	16 bytes	Any value as large as Double
Variant(text)	Length+22 bytes	Same as variable-length string

Table 4.2: Nonnumeric Data Types

4.1.3 Suffixes for Literals

Literals are values that you assign to a data. In some cases, we need to add a suffix behind a literal so that VB2010 can handle the calculation more accurately. For example, we can use num=1.3089# for a Double type data. Some of the suffixes are displayed in Table 4.3.

Suffix	Data Type
&	Long
!	Single
#	Double
@	Currency

Table 4.3: Suffixes for Laterals

In addition, we need to enclose string literals within two quotations and date and time literals within two # sign. Strings can contain any characters, including numbers. The following are few examples:

memberName="Turban, John."
TelNumber="1800-900-888-777"
LastDay=#31-Dec-00#
ExpTime=#12:00 am#

4.2 Managing Variables

Variables are like mail boxes in the post office. The contents of the variables changes every now and then, just like the mail boxes. In term of VB2010, variables are areas allocated by the computer memory to hold data. Like the mail boxes, each variable must be given a name. To name a variable in Visual Basic 2010, you have to follow a set of rules.

4.2.1 Variable Names

The following are the rules when naming the variables in Visual Basic 2010

- ➤ It must be less than 255 characters
- ➤ No spacing is allowed
- ➤ It must not begin with a number
- ➤ Period is not permitted

Examples of valid and invalid variable names are displayed in Table 4.4

Valid Name	Invalid Name	
My_Car	My.Car	
ThisYear	1NewBoy	
Long_Name_Can_beUSE	He&HisFather	*& is not acceptable

Table 4.4: Valid and Invalid Names

4.2.2 Declaring Variables

In Visual Basic 2010, one needs to declare the variables before using them by assigning names and data types. If you fail to do so, the program will show an error. They are normally declared in the general section of the codes' windows using the Dim statement.

The format is as follows:

```
Dim Variable Name As Data Type
```

Example 4.1

```
Private Sub Form1_Load(ByVal sender As System.Object, ByVal e As System.EventArgs) Handles MyBase.Load
```

```
Dim password As String

Dim yourName As String

Dim firstnum As Integer

Dim secondnum As Integer

Dim total As Integer

Dim doDate As Date
```

End Sub

You may also combine them in one line, separating each variable with a comma, as follows:

Dim password As String, yourName As String, firstnum As Integer,.............

For string declaration, there are two possible formats, one for the variable-length string and another for the fixed-length string. For the variable-length string, just use the same format as example 4.1 above. However, for the fixed-length string, you have to use the format as shown below:

Dim VariableName as String * n, where n defines the number of characters the string can hold.

Example 4.2:

Dim yourName as String * 10

yourName can holds no more than 10 Characters.

4.2.3 Assigning Values to Variables

After declaring various variables using the Dim statements, we can assign values to those variables. The general format of an assignment is

Variable=Expression

The variable can be a declared variable or a control property value. The expression could be a mathematical expression, a number, a string, a Boolean value (true or false) and more. The following are some examples:

firstNumber=100

secondNumber=firstNumber-99

userName="John Lyan"

userpass.Text = password

Label1.Visible = True

Command1.Visible = false

Label4.Caption = textbox1.Text

ThirdNumber = Val(usernum1.Text)

total = firstNumber + secondNumber+ThirdNumber

4.3 Constants

Constants are different from variables in the sense that their values do not change during the running of the program.

4.3.1 Declaring a Constant

The format to declare a constant is

Const Constant Name As Data Type = Value

Example 4.3

```
Private Sub Form1_Load(ByVal sender As System.Object, ByVal e As
System.EventArgs) Handles MyBase.Load

        Const Pi As Single=3.142

        Const Temp As Single=37

        Const Score As Single=100

End Sub
```

Summary
- ➢ In section 4.1, you learned that we could categorize data types into numeric and non-numeric data types.
- ➢ In section 4.2, you learned about the rules to name variables in Visual Basic 2010. Besides, you also learned how to declare variables using the Dim keyword and assign values to them.
- ➢ In section 4.3, you learned about constants and the way to declare them.

Chapter 5

Performing Mathematical Operations

❖ Learn how to use Mathematical operators.

Computers can perform mathematical calculations much faster than human beings. However, the computer itself will not be able to perform any mathematical calculations without receiving instructions from the programmer. In VB2010, we can write code to instruct the computer to perform mathematical calculations such as addition, subtraction, multiplication, division and other kinds of arithmetic operations. In order for VB2010 to carry out arithmetic calculations, we need to write code that involves the use of various arithmetic operators. The VB2010 arithmetic operators are very similar to the normal arithmetic operators, only with slight variations. The plus and minus operators are the same while the multiplication operator use the * symbol and the division operator use the / symbol. The list of VB2010 arithmetic operators are shown in table 5.1 below:

Operator	Mathematical function	Example
+	Addition	1+2=3
-	Subtraction	4-1=3
^	Exponential	2^4=16
*	Multiplication	4*3=12, (5*6))2=60
/	Division	12/4=3
Mod	Modulus (return the remainder from an integer division)	15 Mod 4=3 255 mod 10=5
\	Integer Division (discards the decimal places)	19\4=4

Table 5.1: Arithmetic Operators

Example 5.1

In this program, you need to insert two Textboxes, four labels and one button. Click the button and enter the code as shown below. When you run the program, it will perform the four basic arithmetic operations and display the results on the four labels.

```
Private Sub Button1_Click(ByVal sender As System.Object, ByVal e As
System.EventArgs) Handles Button1.Click
        Dim num1, num2, difference, product, quotient As Single
        num1 = TextBox1.Text
        num2 = TextBox2.Text
        sum=num1+num2
        difference=num1-num2
        product = num1 * num2
        quotient=num1/num2
        Label1.Text=sum
        Label2.Text=difference
        Label3.Text = product
        Label4.Text = quotient
End Sub
```

Example 5.2

The program can use Pythagoras Theorem to calculate the length of hypotenuse c given the length of the adjacent side a and the opposite side b. In case you have forgotten the formula for the Pythagoras Theorem, We are showing it below:

$$c^2=a^2+b^2$$

```
Private Sub Button1_Click(ByVal sender As System.Object, ByVal e As
System.EventArgs) Handles Button1.Click
        Dim a, b, c As Single
        a = TextBox1.Text
        b = TextBox2.Text
        c=(a^2+b^2)^(1/2)
        Label3.Text=c
End Sub
```

Example 5.3: BMI Calculator

Many people are obese now and it could affect their health seriously. Obesity has proven by the medical experts to be a one of the main factors that brings many adverse medical problems, including the heart disease.   If your BMI is more than 30, you are considered obese. You can refer to the following range of BMI values for your weight status:

Underweight = <18.5
Normal weight = 18.5-24.9
Overweight = 25-29.9
Obesity = BMI of 30 or greater

In order to calculate your BMI, you do not have to consult your doctor, you could just use a calculator or a homemade computer program, and this is exactly what I am showing you here. The BMI calculator is a Visual Basic program that can calculate the body mass index, or BMI of a person based on the body weight in kilogram and the body height in meter. BMI is calculated based on the formula   weight/ (height)^2, where weight is measured in kg and height in meter. If you only know your weight and height in lb and feet, then you need to convert them to the metric system (you could indeed write a VB program for the conversion).

```
Private Sub Button1_Click (ByVal sender As System.Object, ByVal e As
System.EventArgs) Handles Button1.Click

        Dim height, weight, bmi As Single

        height = TextBox1.Text

        weight = TextBox2.Text

        bmi = (weight) / (height ^ 2)

        Label4.Text = bmi

End Sub
```

The output is shown in the Figure 7-1 below. In this example, your height is 1.80m (about 5 foot 11), your weight is 78 kg(about 170 lb), and your BMI is about 23.5. The reading suggests that you are healthy. (Note; 1 foot=0.3048, 1 lb=.45359237 kilogram)

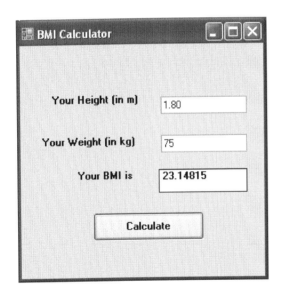

Figure 5.1: BMI Calculator

Summary

In this chapter, you learned how to use various mathematical operators in Visual Basic 2010 in writing code for mathematical calculations. You also learned how to create some programs to solve mathematical problems like Pythagoras Theorem. Besides, you learned how to create the BMI calculator.

Chapter 6

String Manipulation

❖ Learn how to manipulate Strings

String manipulation is an important part of programming because it helps to process data that come in the form of non-numeric types such as name, address, city, book title and etc.

6.1 String Manipulation Using + and & signs.

Strings can be manipulated using the & sign and the + sign, both perform the string concatenation which means combining two or more smaller strings into a larger string. For example, we can join "Visual" and "Basic" into "Visual Basic" using "Visual"&"Basic" or "Visual "+"Basic", as shown in the example below

Example 6.1

```
Public Class Form1

Private Sub Button1_Click(ByVal sender As System.Object, ByVal e As

       System.EventArgs) Handles Button1.Click

       Dim text1, text2, text3 As String

       text1 = "Visual"

       text2 = "Basic"

       text3 = text1 + text2

       Label1.Text = text3

End Sub

End Class
```

The line text3=text1+ text2 can be replaced by text3=text1 & text2 and produced the same output. However, if one of the variables is declared as numeric data type, you cannot use the + sign, you can only use the & sign.

Example 6.2

```
Dim text1, text3 as string

Dim Text2 As Integer

text1 = "Visual"

text2=22

text3=text1+text2

Label1.Text = text3
```

This code will produce an error because of data mismatch. However, using & instead of + will be all right.

Example 6.3

```
Dim text1, text3 as string

Dim Text2 As Integer

text1 = "Visual"

text2=22

text3=text1 & text2

Label1.Text = text3
```

You can combine more than two strings to form a larger string, like the following example:

Example 6.4

```
Private Sub Button1_Click(ByVal sender As System.Object, ByVal e As
System.EventArgs) Handles Button1.Click
        Dim text1, text2, text3, text4, text5, text6 As String
        text1 = "Welcome"
        text2 = " to"
        text3 = " Visual"
        text4 = " Basic"
        text5 = " 2010"
        text6 = text1 + text2 + text3+text4+text5
        Label1.Text = text6
End Sub
```

Running the above program will produce the following screen shot.

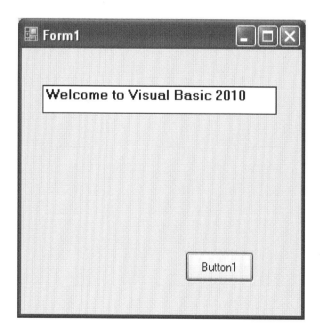

Figure 6.1: The Screen Shot

6.2 String Manipulation Using VB2010 Built-in Functions

A function is similar to a normal procedure but the main purpose of the function is to accept a certain input and return a value, which is passed on to the main program to finish the execution. VB2010 has numerous built-in string manipulation functions but we will only discuss a few here. You will learn more about these functions in later Chapters.

6.2 (a) the Len Function

The length function returns an integer value that is the length of a phrase or a sentence, including the empty spaces. The format is

Len ("Phrase")

For example,

Len (Visual Basic) = 12 and

Len (welcome to VB tutorial) = 22

Example 6.5

```
Public Class Form1

Private Sub Button1_Click(ByVal sender As System.Object, ByVal e As
System.EventArgs) Handles Button1.Click
        Label1.Text = Len(TextBox1.Text)

End Sub
End Class
```

The output is shown in Figure 6.2

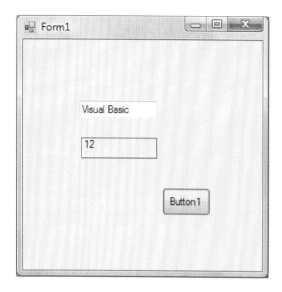

Figure 6.2

6.2(b) the Right Function

The Right function extracts the right portion of a phrase. The format for Visual Basic 6 is

Right ("Phrase", n)

Where n is the starting position from the right of the phase where the portion of the phrase is going to be extracted. For example,

Right("Visual Basic", 4) = asic

However, this format is not applicable in VB2010. In VB2010, we need to use the following format

Microsoft.VisualBasic.Right("Phrase",n)

Example 6.6

```
 Private Sub Button1_Click(ByVal sender As System.Object, ByVal e As
System.EventArgs) Handles Button1.Click

        Dim text1 As String

        text1 = TextBox1.Text

        Label1.Text = Microsoft.VisualBasic.Right(text1, 4)

End Sub
```

The above program will return four right most characters of the phrase entered into the textbox, as shown in Figure 6.3

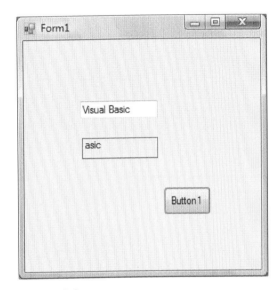

Figure 6.3

*The reason of using the full reference is because many objects have the Right properties so using Right on its own will make it ambiguous to VB2010.

6.2(c) the Left Function

The Left function extract the left portion of a phrase. The format is

```
Microsoft.VisualBasic.Left("Phrase",n)
```

Where n is the starting position from the left of the phase where the portion of the phrase is going to be extracted. For example,

Microsoft.VisualBasic.Left ("Visual Basic", 4) = Visu .

We will learn more about string manipulation function in Chapter 11.

Summary

➢ In section 6.1, you learned how to manipulate strings using + and & signs. The + and & signs are used to join up two strings.

➢ In section 6.2, you learned how to use string manipulation functions. Among the functions are Len, Right and Left,

Chapter 7

Controlling Program Flow

❖ Understanding Conditional and Logical Operators

❖ Using the If control structure with the Comparison Operators

In the previous Chapters, we have learned how to write code that accepts input from the user and displays the output without controlling the program flow. In this chapter, you will learn how to write VB2010 code that can make decision when it processes input from the user, and controls the program flow in the process. Decision making process is an important part of programming because it will help solve practical problems intelligently so that it can provide useful output or feedback to the user. For example, we can write a VB2010 program that can ask the computer to perform certain task until a certain condition is met, or a program that will reject non-numeric data. In order to control the program flow and to make decisions, we need to use the conditional operators and the logical operators together with the If control structure.

7.1 Conditional Operators

The conditional operators are powerful tools that can compare values and then decide what actions to take, whether to execute a program or terminate the program and more. They are also known as numerical comparison operators. Normally we use them to compare two values to see whether they are equal or one value is greater or less than the other value. The comparison will return true or false result. These operators are shown in Table 7.1

Operator	Meaning
=	Equal to
>	More than
<	Less Than
>=	More than and equal
<=	Less than and equal
<>	Not Equal to

Table 7.1: Conditional Operators

7.2 Logical Operators

Sometimes we might need to make more than one comparison before a decision can be made and an action taken. In this case, using numerical comparison operators alone is not sufficient, we need to use additional operators, and they are the logical operators. The logical operators are shown in Table 7.2.

Operator	Meaning
And	Both sides must be true
Or	One side or other must be true
Xor	One side or other must be true but not both
Not	Negates truth

Table 7.2: Logical Operators

* Normally the above operators are use to compare numerical data. However, you can also compare strings with the above operators. In making strings comparison, there are certain rules to follows: Upper case letters are less than lowercase letters, "A"<"B"<"C"<"D"...<"Z" and number are less than letters.

7.3 Using the If control structure with the Comparison Operators

To effectively control the VB program flow, we shall use the **If** control structured together with the conditional operators and logical operators. There are three types of **If** control structure, namely **If...Then** statement, **If...Then... Else** statement and **If...Then...Elself** statement.

7.3(a) If...Then Statement

This is the simplest control structure which ask the computer to perform a certain action specified by the VB expression if the condition is true. However, when the condition is false, no action will be performed. The general format for the if...then... statement is

```
If condition Then

VB expression

End If
```

Example 7.1

```
Private Sub Button1_Click(ByVal sender As System.Object, ByVal e As
System.EventArgs) Handles Button1.Click

        Dim myNumber As Integer
        myNumber = TextBox1.Text
        If myNumber > 100 Then
        Label2.Text = " You win a lucky prize"
        End If

End Sub
```

When you run the program and enter a number that is greater than 100, you will see the "You win a lucky prize" statement. On the other hand, if the number entered is less than or equal to 100, you do not see any display.

7.3(b) If...Then...Else Statement

Using just If...Then statement is not very useful in programming and it does not provides choices for the users. In order to provide a choice, we can use the If...Then...Else Statement. This control structure will ask the computer to perform a certain action specified by the VB expression if the condition is true. When the condition is false, an alternative action will be executed. The general format for if...then... Else statement is

```
If condition Then

VB expression

Else

VB expression

End If
```

Example 7.2

```
Private Sub Button1_Click(ByVal sender As System.Object, ByVal e As
System.EventArgs) Handles Button1.Click

        Dim myNumber As Integer
        myNumber = TextBox1.Text
        If myNumber > 100 Then
        Label2.Text = "Congratulation! You win a lucky prize!"
        Else
        Label2.Text = "Sorry, You did not win any prize"
        End If

End Sub
```

When you run the program and enter a number that is greater than 100, it displays a message "Congratulation! You win a lucky prize!" On the other hand, if the number entered is less than or equal to 100, you will see the "Sorry, You did not win any prize" message.

Example 7.3

```
Private Sub Button1_Click(ByVal sender As System.Object, ByVal e As
System.EventArgs) Handles Button1.Click

        Dim myNumber, MyAge As Integer
        myNumber = TextBox1.Text
        MyAge = TextBox2.Text

        If myNumber > 100 And myAge > 60 Then
        Label2.Text = " Congratulation! You win a lucky prize"
        Else
        Label2.Text = " Sorry, You did not win any prize"
        End If

End Sub
```

This program use the logical **And** operator beside the conditional operators. This means that for the statement to be true, both conditions must be fulfilled in order; otherwise, the second block of code will be executed. In this example, the number entered must be more than 100 and the age must be more than 60 in order to win a lucky prize, any one of the above conditions not fulfilled will disqualify the user from winning a prize.

7.3(c) If...Then...ElseIf Statement

If there are more than two alternatives, using just If...Then...Else statement will not be enough. In order to provide more choices, we can use the If...Then...ElseIf Statement. The general format for the if...then... Else statement is

```
If condition Then
VB expression
ElseIf condition Then
VB expression
ElseIf condition Then
VB expression
Else
      VB expression
End If
```

Example 7.4

```
Private Sub Button1_Click(ByVal sender As System.Object, ByVal e As
System.EventArgs) Handles Button1.Click
Dim Mark As Integer
Dim Grade as String
Mark = TextBox1.Text
If myNumber >=80 Then
Grade="A"
ElseIf Mark>=60 and Mark<80 then
Grade="B"
ElseIf Mark>=40 and Mark<60 then
Grade="C"
Else
Grade="D"
End If
End Sub
```

Summary

In this chapter, you learned how to use the If control structure together with the comparison operators to control program flow.

➤ In section 7.1, you learned how to use the conditional operators in VB2010 such as =, <,>, >=, <= and <>.

➤ In section 7.2, you learned how to use the logical operators And, Or, Xor and Not.

➤ In section 7.3, you learned how to implement three types of If control structure, i.e. If...Then, If...Then...Else and If...Then...ElseIf.

Chapter 8

Select Case Control Structure

❖ Understanding the Select Case ....End Select Structure

In the previous Chapter, we have learned how to control the program flow using the If...Elself control structure. In this chapter, you will learn another way to control the program flow, that is, the Select Case control structure. However, the Select Case control structure is slightly different from the If...Elself control structure. The difference is that the Select Case control structure basically only make decision on one expression or dimension (for example the examination grade) while the If...Elself statement control structure may evaluate only one expression, each If...Elself statement may also compute entirely different dimensions. Select Case is preferred when there exist many different conditions because using If...Then...Elself statements might become too messy. The Select Case ...End Select control structure is shown below:

Select Case test expression

   Case expression list 1

      Block of one or more VB statements

   Case expression list 2

      Block of one or more VB Statements

   Case expression list 3

      Block of one or more VB statements

   Case expression list 4

       Block of one or more VB statements

   Case Else

      Block of one or more VB Statements

End Select

Example 8.1

Based on Example 7.4, you can rewrite the code using Select Case...End Select, as shown below.

```
Private Sub Button1_Click(ByVal sender As System.Object, ByVal e As
System.EventArgs) Handles Button1.Click

'Examination Marks

Dim mark As Single
 mark = mrk.Text
Select Case mark

 Case 0 to 49
     Label1.Text = "Need to work harder"
  Case 50 to 59
     Label2.Text = "Average"
  Case 60 to 69

   Label3.Text= "Above Average"

  Case 70 to 84
Label4.Text = "Good"
 Case Else
Label5.Text= "Excellence"
End Select

 End Sub
```

Example 8.2

In this example, you can use the keyword **Is** together with the comparison operators.

```
Private Sub Button1_Click (ByVal sender As System.Object, ByVal e As
System.EventArgs) Handles Button1.Click


'Examination Marks

Dim mark As Single
mark = mrk.Text

Select Case mark
Case Is >= 85

    Label1.Text= "Excellence"
Case Is >= 70

    Label2.Text= "Good"


Case Is >= 60
   Label3.Text = "Above Average"


Case Is >= 50
Label4.Text= "Average"

Case Else
Label5.Text = "Need to work harder"
End Select

End Sub
```

Example 8.3

You also can rewrite Example 8.2 by omitting the keyword IS, as shown here:

```
Private Sub Button1_Click(ByVal sender As System.Object, ByVal e As
System.EventArgs) Handles Button1.Click
```

```
'Examination Marks
Dim mark As Single


mark = mrk.Text


Select Case mark
 Case 0 to 49
     Label1.Text = "Need to work harder"
 Case 50 to 59
     Label2.Text = "Average"
 Case 60 to 69
     Label3.Text= "Above Average"
 Case 70 to 84
     Label4.Text = "Good"
 Case Else
     Label5.Text= "Excellence"
End Select


End Sub
```

Summary

In this chapter, you learned how to control program flow using the Select Case control structure. You also learned how to write code for the practical usage of the Select Case control structure, such as the program that processed examination marks.

Chapter 9

Looping

❖ Understanding and using For... Next Loop

❖ Understanding and using Do...Loop

❖ Understanding and using While...End while Loop

Visual Basic 2010 allows a procedure to repeat many times as long as the processor could support. We call this looping. Looping is required when we need to process something repetitively until a certain condition is met. For example, we can design a program that adds a series of numbers until it exceed a certain value, or a program that asks the user to enter data repeatedly until he or she keys in the word 'Finish'. In Visual Basic 2010, we have three types of Loops, they are the **For...Next** loop, the **Do loop** and the **While...End while** loop

9.1 For...Next Loop

The format is:

For counter=startNumber to endNumber (Step increment)

   One or more VB statements

Next

Sometimes the user might want to get out from the loop before the whole repetitive process is completed. The command to use is **Exit For**. To exit a For....Next Loop, you can place the Exit For statement within the loop; and it is normally used together with the If.....Then... statement. For its application, you can refer to Example 9.1 d.

Example 9.1 a

```
Dim counter as Integer

For  counter=1 to 10

ListBox1.Items.Add (counter)

 Next
```

* The program will enter number 1 to 10 into the Listbox.

Example 9.1b

```
Dim counter , sum As Integer

For counter=1  to 100 step 10

sum+=counter

ListBox1.Items.Add (sum)

 Next
```

* The program will calculate the sum of the numbers as follows:
 sum=0+10+20+30+40+......

Example 9.1c

```
Dim counter, sum As Integer

sum = 1000

For counter = 100 To 5 Step -5

sum - = counter

ListBox1.Items.Add(sum)

Next
```

*Notice that increment can be negative.

The program will compute the subtraction as follows: 1000-100-95-90-..........

Example 9.1d

```
Dim n as Integer

For n=1 to 10

 If n>6 then

Exit For

End If

Else

ListBox1.Items.Add ( n)

Next

End If

Next
```

The process will stop when n is greater than 6.

9.2 Do Loop

The formats are

a) Do While condition
        Block of one or more VB statements
    Loop

b) Do
        Block of one or more VB statements
    Loop While condition

c) Do Until condition
        Block of one or more VB statements
    Loop

d) Do
        Block of one or more VB statements
    Loop Until condition

Example 9.2(a)

```
Do while counter <=1000
    TextBox1.Text=counter
    counter +=1
Loop
```

* The above example will keep on adding until counter >1000. This example can be rewritten as

```
Do
    TextBox1.Text=counter
    counter+=1
Loop until counter>1000
```

Sometime we need exit to exit a loop prematurely because of a certain condition is fulfilled.

The syntax we use is Exit Do. Let us examine the following example:

Example 9.2(b)

```
Private Sub Button1_Click(ByVal sender As System.Object, ByVal e As
System.EventArgs) Handles Button1.Click
    Dim sum, n As Integer
    Do
    n += 1
    sum += n
    ListBox1.Items.Add(n & vbTab & sum)
    If n = 100 Then
    Exit Do
    End If
    Loop

    End Sub
```

In the above Example, we find the summation of 1+2+3+4+......+100. In the design stage, you need to insert a ListBox into the form for displaying the output, named List1. The program uses the **Add** method to populate the ListBox. The statement ListBox1.Items.Add (n & vbTab & sum) will display the headings in the ListBox, where it uses the vbTab function to create a space between the headings n and sum.

9.3 While ...End While Loop

The structure of a While....End While is very similar to the Do Loop. It takes the following format:

While condition

    Statements

End While

Example 9.3

```
Private Sub Button1_Click(ByVal sender As System.Object, ByVal e As
System.EventArgs) Handles Button1.Click
        Dim sum, n As Integer
        While n <> 100
        n += 1
        sum = sum + n
        ListBox1.Items.Add(n & vbTab & sum)
        End While
End Sub
```

Summary
> In section 9.1, you learned how to write code for the For...Next loop. The loop stops when a condition is met. You also learned how to use Exit For to exit the loop.
> In section 9.2, you learned how to write code for the Do loop procedure. You also learned how to use Exit Do to exit the loop.
> In section 9.3, you learned how to write code for the While...End While loop. You also learned that the loop stops when a condition is met.

Chapter 10

Introduction to Functions

❖ Getting to know all the functions in Visual Basic 2010

A function is similar to a normal procedure but the main purpose of the function is to accept a certain input and return a value, which is passed on to the main program to finish the execution. There are two types of functions, the built-in functions (or internal functions) and the functions created by the programmers. The general format of a function is

FunctionName (arguments)

The arguments are values that are passed on to the function.

In this Chapter, we are going to learn two very basic but useful internal functions of Visual Basic, i.e. the MsgBox( ) and InputBox ( ) functions.

10.1 MsgBox ( ) Function

The objective of MsgBox is to produce a pop-up message box and prompt the user to click on a command button before he /she can continues. This format is as follows:

yourMsg=MsgBox(Prompt, Style Value, Title)

The first argument, Prompt, displays the message in the message box. The Style Value determines the type of command buttons appear on the message box, as shown in Table 10.1. The Title argument displays the title of the message board.

Style Value	Named Constant	Buttons Displayed
0	vbOkOnly	Ok button
1	vbOkCancel	Ok and Cancel buttons
2	vbAbortRetryIgnore	Abort, Retry and Ignore buttons.
3	vbYesNoCancel	Yes, No and Cancel buttons
4	vbYesNo	Yes and No buttons
5	vbRetryCancel	Retry and Cancel buttons

Table 10.1: Style Values

We can use named constant in place of integers for the second argument to make the programs more readable. In fact, VB6 will automatically shows up a list of names constant where you can select one of them.

For example,

yourMsg=MsgBox("Click OK to Proceed", 1, "Startup Menu")

 and

yourMsg=Msg("Click OK to Proceed". vbOkCancel,"Startup Menu")

are the same.

yourMsg is a variable that holds values that are returned by the MsgBox ( ) function. The type of buttons being clicked by the users determines the values. It has to be declared as Integer data type in the procedure or in the general declaration section. Table 10.2 shows the values, the corresponding named constant and buttons.

Value	Named Constant	Button Clicked
1	vbOk	Ok button
2	vbCancel	Cancel button
3	vbAbort	Abort button
4	vbRetry	Retry button
5	vbIgnore	Ignore button
6	vbYes	Yes button
7	vbNo	No button

Table 10.2: Return Values and Command Buttons

A function is similar to a normal procedure but the main purpose of the function is to accept a certain input and return a value, which is passed on to the main program to finish the execution. There are two types of functions, the built-in functions (or internal functions) and the functions created by the programmers.

The general format of a function is

FunctionName (arguments)

The arguments are values that are passed on to the function.

Example 10.1

```
Private Sub Button1_Click(ByVal sender As System.Object, ByVal e As
System.EventArgs) Handles Button1.Click
Dim testmsg As Integer
testmsg = MsgBox("Click to test", 1, "Test message")
If testmsg = 1 Then
MessageBox.Show("You have clicked the OK button")
Else
MessageBox.Show("You have clicked the Cancel button")
End If
End Sub
```

To make the message box looks more sophisticated, you can add an icon besides the message. There are four types of icons available in VB2010 as shown in Table 10.3

Value	Named Constant	Icon
16	vbCritical	
32	vbQuestion	
48	vbExclamation	
64	vbInformation	

Table 10.3: Named Constants and Icons

Example 10.2

Private Sub Button1_Click(ByVal sender As System.Object, ByVal e As

System.EventArgs) Handles Button1.Click

Dim testMsg As Integer

testMsg = MsgBox("Click to Test", vbYesNoCancel + vbExclamation, "Test Message")

If testMsg = 6 Then

MessageBox.Show("You have clicked the yes button")

ElseIf testMsg = 7 Then

MessageBox.Show("You have clicked the NO button")

Else

MessageBox.Show("You have clicked the Cancel button")

End If

End Sub

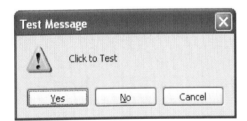

Figure 10.1

10.2 The InputBox( ) Function

An InputBox( ) function allows the user to enter a value or a message in a text box.

userMsg =Microsoft.VisualBasic.InputBox(Prompt, Title, default_text, x-position, y-position)

userMsg is a variant data type but typically, it is declared as string, which accepts the message input by the user. The meanings of the arguments:

- Prompt   - Message displayed by the InputBox, normally as a question.
- Title   - Title of the InputBox.
- default-text - The default text or value that appears in the input field where the user may change it according to his or her wish..
- x-position and y-position - the position or the coordinates of the InputBox.

Example 10.3

```
Private Sub Button1_Click(ByVal sender As System.Object, ByVal e As

System.EventArgs) Handles Button1.Click

Dim userMsg As String

userMsg = Microsoft.VisualBasic.InputBox("What is your message?", "Message Entry

Form", "Enter your message here", 500, 700)

If userMsg <> "" Then

MessageBox.Show(userMsg)

Else

MessageBox.Show("No Message")

End If

End Sub
```

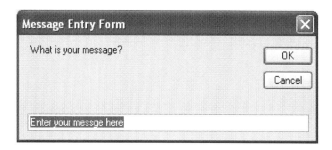

Figure 10.2

Summary

You learned that a function is a procedure that accepts an input and returns a value, which is passed on to the main program to finish the execution. You also learned that the format of a function is FunctionName (arguments).

➤ In section 10.1, you learned to use the Msg () function to produce a popup message box to prompt the user to click on a button to continue the execution.

In section 10.2, you learned how to use the InputBox to get the input from the user.

Chapter 11

String Functions

We have learned about the basic concept of function as well as the MsgBox and InputBox functions in Chapter 10. I. In fact, I have already shown you a few string manipulation functions in Chapter 6; they are the Len function, the Left function and the Right Function. In this Chapter, we will learn other string manipulation functions.

11.1 The Mid Function

The Mid function is to retrieve a part of text from a given phrase. The format of the Mid Function is

Mid(phrase, position,n)

Where **phrase** is the string from which a part of text is to be retrieved, **position** is the starting position of the phrase from which the retrieving process begins and **n** is the number of characters to retrieve.

Example 11.1

```
Private Sub Button1_Click(ByVal sender As System.Object, ByVal e As
System.EventArgs) Handles Button1.Click

    Dim myPhrase As String
    myPhrase = Microsoft.VisualBasic.InputBox("Enter your phrase")
    Label1.Text = Mid(myPhrase, 2, 6)

End Sub
```

In this example, when the user clicks the command button, an input box will pop up asking the user to input a phrase. After a phrase is entered and the OK button is pressed, the label will show the extracted text starting from position 2 of the phrase and the number of characters extracted is 6, as shown in Figure 11.1 and Figure 11.2

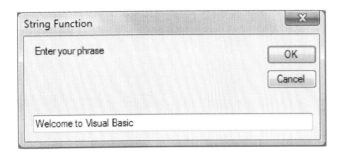

Figure 11.1

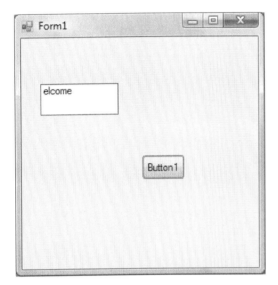

Figure 11.2

11.2 The Right Function

The Right function extracts the right portion of a phrase. The format is

Microsoft.Visualbasic.Right ("Phrase", n)

Where n is the starting position from the right of the phase where the portion of the phrase is to be extracted. For example:

Microsoft.Visualbasic.Right ("Visual Basic", 4) = asic

For example, you can write the following code to extract the right portion any phrase entered by the user.

```
Private Sub Button1_Click (ByVal sender As System.Object, ByVal e As

System.EventArgs) Handles Button1.Click

    Dim myword As String

    myword = TextBox1.Text

    Label1.Text = Microsoft.VisualBasic.Right (myword, 4)

End Sub
```

The output is shown in Figure 11.3

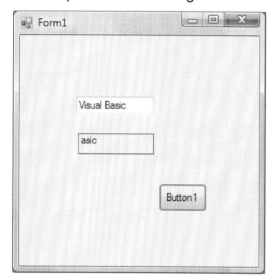

Figure 11.3

11.3 The Left Function

The Left function extracts the Left portion of a phrase. The format is

Microsoft.Visualbasic.Left ("Phrase", n)

Where n is the starting position from the right of the phase where the portion of the phrase is going to be extracted. For example:

Microsoft.Visualbasic.Left ("Visual Basic", 4) = Visu

For example, you can write the following code to extract the left portion any phrase entered by the user.

```
Private Sub Button1_Click (ByVal sender As System.Object, ByVal e As
System.EventArgs) Handles Button1.Click
    Dim myword As String
    myword = TextBox1.Text
    Label1.Text = Microsoft.VisualBasic.Left (myword, 4)
End Sub
```

The output is shown in Figure 11.4

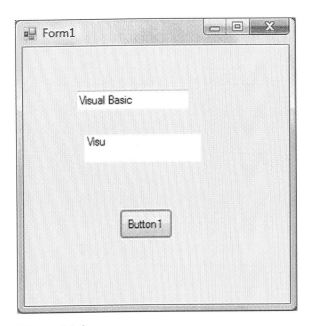

Figure 11.4:

11.4 The Trim Function

The Trim function trims the empty spaces on both side of the phrase. The format is
Trim("Phrase")
.For example,

Trim ("   Visual Basic   ") = Visual basic

Example 11.2

```
Private Sub Button1_Click(ByVal sender As System.Object, ByVal e As
System.EventArgs) Handles Button1.Click
Dim myPhrase As String
myPhrase = Microsoft.VisualBasic.InputBox("Enter your phrase")
Label1.Text = Trim(myPhrase)
End Sub
```

11.5 The Ltrim Function

The Ltrim function trims the empty spaces of the left portion of the phrase. The format is

Ltrim("Phrase")

.For example,

Ltrim ("   Visual Basic")= Visual basic

11.6 The Rtrim Function

The Rtrim function trims the empty spaces of the right portion of the phrase. The format is

Rtrim("Phrase")

.For example,

Rtrim ("Visual Basic   ") = Visual Basic

11.7 The InStr function

The InStr function looks for a phrase that is embedded within the original phrase and returns the starting position of the embedded phrase. The format is

Instr (n, original phase, embedded phrase)

Where n Is the position where the Instr function will begin to look for the embedded phrase.

For example

Instr(1, "Visual Basic"," Basic")=8

The function returns a numeric value.

You can write a program code as shown below:

Private Sub Button1_Click(ByVal sender As System.Object, ByVal e As

System.EventArgs) Handles Button1.Click

Label1.Text = InStr(1, "Visual Basic", "Basic")

End Sub

11.8 The Ucase and the Lcase Functions

The Ucase function converts all the characters of a string to capital letters. On the other hand, the Lcase function converts all the characters of a string to small letters.
The format is

Microsoft.VisualBasic.UCase(Phrase)

Microsoft.VisualBasic.LCase(Phrase)

For example,

Microsoft.VisualBasic.Ucase ("Visual Basic") =VISUAL BASIC

Microsoft.VisualBasic.Lcase ("Visual Basic") =visual basic

11.9 The Chr and the Asc functions

The Chr function returns the string that corresponds to an ASCII code while the Asc function converts an ASCII character or symbol to the corresponding ASCII code. ASCII stands for "American Standard Code for Information Interchange". Altogether there are 255 ASCII codes and as many ASCII characters. Some of the characters may not be displayed as they may represent some actions such as the pressing of a key or produce a beep sound. The format of the Chr function is

Chr(charcode)

in addition, the format of the Asc function is

Asc(Character)

The following are some examples:

Chr(65)=A, Chr(122)=z, Chr(37)=% ,

Asc("B")=66, Asc("&")=38

* For the complete set of ASCII , please refer to Appendix I

Summary

In this chapter, you learned how to use various string manipulation functions.

> In section 11.1, you learned how to use the Mid function to retrieve a part of text from a phrase.

> In section 11.2, you learned how to use the Right function to extracts the right portion of a phrase.

> In section 11.3, you learned how to use the left function to extracts the left portion of a phrase

> In section 11.4, you learned how to use the Trim function to trims the empty spaces on both side of the phrase.

> In section 11.5, you learned how to use the Ltrim function to trim the empty spaces of the left portion of the phrase.

> In section 11.6, you learned how to use the Rtrim function to trim empty spaces of the right portion of the phrase.

> In section 11.7, you learned how to use the InStr function looks for a phrase that is embedded within the original phrase and returns the starting position of the embedded phrase.

> In Section 11.8, you learned how to use the Ucase function to convert all the characters of a string to capital letters and the Lcase function to convert all the characters of a string to small letters.

> In section 11.9, you learned how to use the Chr function to return the string that corresponds to an ASCII code and the Asc function to convert an ASCII character or symbol to the corresponding ASCII code

Chapter 12

Mathematical Functions

❖ Learning How to use the Mathematical functions

We have learned how to write code to perform mathematical calculations using standard mathematical operators. However, we need to use the built-in Math functions in VB2010 to handle complex mathematical calculations. Math functions are methods that belong to the Math Class of the .Net framework. They are similar to the math functions in Visual Basic 6. The Math functions in VB2010 are Abs, Exp, Fix, Int, Log, Rnd(), Round and the trigonometric functions.

12.1 The Abs function

The Abs returns the absolute value of a given number.

The syntax is

Math. Abs (number)

The **Math** keyword here indicates that the Abs function belongs to the Math class. However, not all mathematical functions belong to the Math class.

12.2 The Exp function

The Exp of a number x is the exponential value of x, i.e. e^x.

For example, Exp(1)=e=2.71828182

The syntax is

Math.Exp (number)

Example 12.2

Private Sub Button1_Click(ByVal sender As System.Object, ByVal e As System.EventArgs) Handles Button1.Click

```
Dim num1, num2 As Single
num1 = TextBox1.Text
num2 = Math.Exp(num1)
Label1.Text = num2
```

End Sub

12.3 The Fix Function

The Fix function truncates the decimal part of a positive number and returns the largest integer smaller than the number. However, when the number is negative, it will return smallest integer larger than the number. For example, Fix (9.2)=9 but Fix(-9.4)=-9

Example 12.3

Private Sub Button1_Click(ByVal sender As System.Object, ByVal e As System.EventArgs) Handles Button1.Click

```
Dim num1, num2 As Single
num1 = TextBox1.Text
num2 = Fix(num1)
Label1.Text = num2
```

End Sub

12.4 The Int Function

The Int is a function that converts a number into an integer by truncating its decimal part and the resulting integer is the largest integer that is smaller than the number. For example

Int(2.4)=2, Int(6.9)=6 , Int(-5.7)=-6, Int(-99.8)=-100

12.5 The Log Function

The Log function is the function that returns the natural logarithm of a number. For example, Log(10)=2.302585

Example 12.4

```
Private Sub Button1_Click(ByVal sender As System.Object, ByVal e As
System.EventArgs) Handles Button1.Click

        Dim num1, num2 As Single
        num1 = TextBox1.Text
        num2 = Math.Log(num1)
        Label1.Text = num2

End Sub
```

* Label1 shows the value of logarithm of num1.

12.6 The Rnd( ) Function

The Rnd is very useful when we deal with the concept of chance and probability. The Rnd function returns a random value between 0 and 1. Random numbers in their original form are not very useful in programming until we convert them to integers. For example, if we need to obtain a random output of 6 integers ranging from 1 to 6, which makes the program behave like a virtual dice, we need to convert the random numbers to integers using the formula Int(Rnd*6)+1.

Example 12.5

Private Sub Button1_Click (ByVal sender As System.Object, ByVal e As System.EventArgs) Handles Button1.Click

    Dim num as integer

    Randomize ( )

    Num=Int(Rnd()*6)+1

    Label1.Text=Num

End Sub

In this example, Int(Rnd*6) will generate a random integer between 0 and 5 because the function **Int** truncates the decimal part of the random number and returns an integer. After adding 1, you will get a random number between 1 and 6 every time you click the command button. For example, let say the random number generated is 0.98, after multiplying it by 6, it becomes 5.88, and using the integer function Int(5.88) will convert the number to 5; and after adding 1 you will get 6.

12.7 The Round Function

The **Round** function rounds up a number to a certain number of decimal places. The Format is Round (n, m) which means to round a number n to m decimal places. For example, Math.Round (7.2567, 2) =7.26

Example 12.6

```
Private Sub Button1_Click(ByVal sender As System.Object, ByVal e As
System.EventArgs) Handles Button1.Click

        Dim num1, num2 As Single
        num1 = TextBox1.Text
        num2 = Math.Round(num1, 2)
        Label1.Text = num2

End Sub
```

12.8 The Sqrt Function

The Sqrt function returns the square root of a number. For example, Sqrt(400) will return a value of 20. You can use this function to solve problems related to Pythagoras theorem. For exam, you may want to find the length of the hypotenuse given the length of the adjacent side and the length of the opposite side of a triangle. The code in VB2010 is:

```
c=Math.Sqrt(a^2+b^2)
```

*As Sqrt is a function that belongs to the Math class, we need to use the Math keyword.

The following code computes the hypotenuse c given the length of adjacent side and the length of the opposite side of triangle.

```
Private Sub Button1_Click(ByVal sender As System.Object, ByVal e As
System.EventArgs) Handles Button1.Click
        Dim a, b, c As Single
        a = Val(TxtA.Text)
        b = Val(TxtB.Text)
```

```
c = Math.Sqrt(a ^ 2 + b ^ 2)

LblC.Text = c.ToString("F")

End Sub
```

The above project requires two text boxes and five label controls. One of the label controls is for displaying the results of the calculation.

The output image looks something like in Figure 12.1

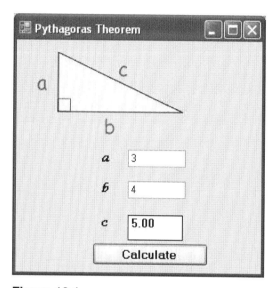

Figure 12.1

12.9 Trigonometric Functions

Trigonometric functions handle problems involving angles. The basic trigonometric functions in Visual Basic 2010 are Sin, Cos, Tan and Atan. Sin is the function that returns the value of sine of an angle in radian, Cos returns the value of cosine of an angle in radian and Tan returns the value of tangent of an angle in radian. Atan returns the value of Arc tangent, which represents the value of the angle in radian given the value of tangent of this angle. Arc tangent is expressed as $\tan^{-1}(x) = y$, which means $\tan(y) = x$. For example, $\tan^{-1}(1) = \frac{\pi}{4}$.

If you wish to accept input in degree from the user, you need to convert degree to radian using the following formula:

$$1 \text{ degree} = \frac{\pi}{180}$$

The first code you should write before you can values of trigonometric functions is the function to compute the value of π, or Pi. We use the fact that $\tan^{-1}(1) = \frac{\pi}{4}$, which is Atan $(1) = \frac{\text{Pi}}{4}$ in VB language to obtain the formula Pi= 4 xAtan (1). Therefore, the code to get value of Pi is as follows:

```
Public Function Pi( ) As Double
      Return 4.0 * Math.Atan(1.0)
    End Function
```

We use the keyword Public as we wish to use the value of Pi throughout the module.

In the following example, we will show you how to obtain the values of Sine, Cosine and Tangent of an angle.

Example 12.7

In this example, the program allows the user to enter an angle in degree and calculate the values of sine, cosine and tangent of this angle. Start a new project and name it Trigo Functions. Next, insert one text box into the form and name it as TxtAngle. The purpose of the text box is allowing the user to enter an angle in degree. You also add three labels and name them as LblSin, LblCos and LblTan to display the values of sine, cosine and tangent of the angle. Insert four other labels for labeling purpose. Lastly, add one button and name it as BtnCal.

First, under the statement Public Class Form1 enter the code to compute the value of Pi as follows:

```
Public Function Pi() As Double

    ' Calculate the value of pi.

        Return 4.0 * Math.Atan(1.0)

    End Function
```

Next, click on the button and enter the following code:

```
 Private Sub BtnCal_Click(ByVal sender As System.Object, ByVal e As
System.EventArgs) Handles BtnCal.Click
    Dim degree As Single, angle As Double
    degree = TxtAngle.Text
    angle = degree * (Pi() / 180)
    LblSin.Text = Math.Sin(angle).ToString("F")
    LblCos.Text = Math.Cos(angle).ToString("F")
    LblTan.Text = Math.Tan(angle).ToString("F")


  End Sub
```

The output interface is shown in Figure 12.2

Figure 12.2

Example 12.8

This example computes the area and circumference of a circle. The formula of area of circle is πr^2 and the formula of circumference is $2\pi r$. In this program, you insert a text box to allow the user to enter the value of radius of the circle. Add two labels to display the value of Area and the value of circumference. Use the ToString method to specify number of decimal places with the F specifier. F3 means three decimal places and F alone means two decimal places.

```
Public Function Pi() As Double

      Return 4.0 * Math.Atan(1.0)

   End Function

   Private Sub Form1_Load(ByVal sender As System.Object, ByVal e As

   System.EventArgs) Handles MyBase.Load

   End Sub

   Private Sub TxtRadius_TextChanged (ByVal sender As System.Object, ByVal e

   As System.EventArgs) Handles TxtRadius.TextChanged

      Dim r, l, Area As Double
```

```
    r = Val(TxtRadius.Text)

    l = 2 * Pi() * r

    Area = Pi() * r ^ 2

    LblCirCumF.Text = l.ToString("F")

    LblArea.Text = Area.ToString("F3")
End Sub
```

The runtime interface is shown in Figure 12.3

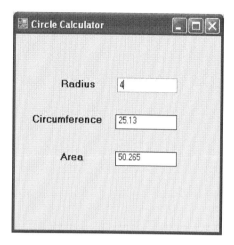

Figure 12.2

Summary

In this chapter, you learned how to write code to perform calculations using various built-in mathematical functions in VB2010.

➢ In section 12.1, you learned how to use the Abs function to return the absolute value of a given number.

➢ In section 12.2, you learned how to use the Exp function to express a number in exponential form.

➢ In section 12.3, you learned how to use the Fix function to truncate the decimal part of a positive number and return the largest integer smaller than the number.

➢ In section 12.4, you learned how to use the Int function to convert a number into an integer by truncating its decimal part and the resulting integer is the largest integer that is smaller than the number.

➢ In section 12.5, you learned how to use the Log function to return value of the natural logarithm of a number

➢ In section 12.6, you learned how to use the Rnd( ) function to generate a random value between 0 and 1.

➢ In section 12.7, you learned how to use Round function to round up a number to a certain number of decimal places.

➢ In Section 12.8, you learned how to use the Sqrt function to obtain the square root of a number.

➢ In section 12.9, you learned how to use the trigonometric functions Sin, Cos and Tan to compute the values of sine, cosine and tangent of an angle in radian. You also learned how to obtain the value of Pi using the formula Pi=4xAtan(1)

Chapter 13

Formatting Functions

❖ Learning how to use the Formatting Functions

13.1 Format Function

The **Format** function is a very powerful formatting function that can display the numeric values in various forms. There are two types of Format function, one of them is the built-in or predefined format, and the user can define another one.

(i) The format of the predefined Format function is

Format (n, "style")

Where n is a number and the list of style arguments is given in Table 13.1

Style	Explanation	Example
General Number	Displays the number without having separators between thousands	Format(8972.234, "General Number")=8972.234
Fixed	Displays the number without having separators between thousands and rounds it up to two decimal places.	Format(8972.2, "Fixed")=8972.23
Standard	Displays the number with separators or separators between thousands and rounds it up to two decimal places.	Format(6648972.265, "Standard")= 6,648,972.27
Currency	Displays the number with the dollar sign in front, shows separators between thousands and rounding it up to two decimal places.	Format(6648972.265, "Currency")= $6,648,972.27
Percent	Converts the number to the percentage form, displays a % sign, and rounds it up to two decimal places.	Format(0.56324, "Percent")=56.32 %

Table 13.1: The Format Function

Example 13.1

Private Sub Button1_Click(ByVal sender As System.Object, ByVal e As

System.EventArgs) Handles Button1.Click, Button5.Click, Button4.Click, Button3.Click

Label1.Text = Format(8972.234, "General Number")

Label2.Text = Format(8972.2, "Fixed")

Label3.Text = Format(6648972.265, "Standard")

Label4.Text = Format(6648972.265, "Currency")

Label5.Text = Format(0.56324, "Percent")

End Sub

The output window is shown below:

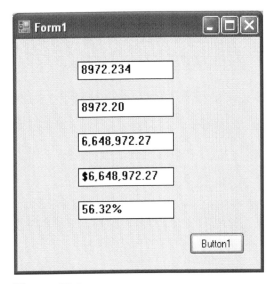

Figure 13.1

(ii) The format of the user-defined Format function is

Format (n, "user's format")

Although it is known as user-defined format, we still need to follow certain formatting styles. Examples of user-defined formatting style are listed in Table 13.2

Example	Explanation	Output
Format(781234.57,"0")	Rounds to whole number without separators between thousands	781235
Format(781234.57,"0.0")	Rounds to one decimal place without separators between thousands	781234.6
Format(781234.576,"0.00")	Rounds to two decimal places without separators between thousands	781234.58
Format(781234.576,"#,##0.00")	Rounds to two decimal places with separators between thousands	781,234.58
Format(781234.576,"$#,##0.00")	Shows dollar sign and rounds to 2 decimal places with separators between thousands	$781,234.58
Format(0.576,"0%")	Converts to percentage form without decimal places.	58%
Format(0.5768,"0.00%")	Converts to percentage form with 2 decimal places	57.68%

Table 13.2: User's Defined Functions

Example 13.2

```
Private Sub Button1_Click(ByVal sender As System.Object, ByVal e As
System.EventArgs) Handles Button1.Click, Button5.Click, Button4.Click, Button3.Click
Label1.Text = Format(8972.234, "0.0")
Label2.Text = Format(8972.2345, "0.00")
Label3.Text = Format(6648972.265, "#,##0.00")
Label4.Text = Format(6648972.265, "$#,##0.00")
Label5.Text = Format(0.56324, "0%")
End Sub
```

The output window is shown in Figure 13.2:

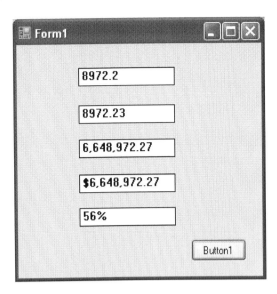

Figure 13.2: User's Defined Functions

13.2 Formatting Using ToString Method

Other than using the Format function, VB.Net has introduced the ToString method to format output. It is used together with the standard numeric format specifiers such as "c" which stand for currency. Some of the most common numeric specifiers are listed in the Table 13.3.

Format specifier	Explanation	Examples
"C"	i) Displays a currency value. The default is the US currency $ and in two decimal places. ii) To display other currency, add a culture code that specifies a country. For example, for Great Britain, you add en-GB using the keyword "CultureInfo.	**Dim myNum as Single =2011.123456** myNum.ToString("C")= $2011.12 myNum.ToString("C4")= $2011.1234 myNum.ToString("C3", CultureInfo. CreateSpecificCulture("en-GB"))= £2011.123

	CreateSpecificCulture" iii) Displays number of decimal digits by placing the digit after C, for example, C4 for decimal places.	
"D" or "d"	Express a Number with in integer form with specified number of digits. For example, D4 means four-digit integer.	Dim myNumber As Integer = 2012.2344 myNumber.ToString("D4")=2012
"E" or "e"	Express a number in exponential form with specified number of decimal places	Dim myNumber As Double = 2012.2344 myNumber.ToString("e3")= 2.012e+003
"P" or "p"	Multiply a number by 100 and displayed with a percentage symbol % .	Dim myNumber As Double = 0.23456 myNumber.ToString("P2")= 23.46%
"F" or "f"	Specifies number of decimal points	Dim myNumber As Double=0.23456 myNumber.ToString("F")=0.23 myNumber.ToString("F3")=0.235

Table 13.3: Standard numeric format specifiers

The ToString method together with the currency specifier "C" displays the output with the currency sign $ and in two decimal places. The default currency is the currency used by your computer system; in this case, it is the US currency. If you are not sure of what default currency your computer uses, you can add the keyword "CultureInfo.CurrentCulture" to the ToString method as shown in the example below:

```
FutureValue = FV.ToString("C", CultureInfo.CurrentCulture)
```

If you wish to display the output in different currencies, you can use the keyword" "CultureInfo.CreateSpecificCulture together with the culture identifiers. For example, if you want to display the output in Japanese currency, you can use the ja-JP culture identifier, as shown in the example below:

```
FutureValue = FV.ToString("C", CultureInfo. CreateSpecificCulture("ja-JP")
```

The output is in Japanese currency sign ¥ instead of the $ sign.

Summary

In this chapter, you learned how to format your output using the Format and the ToString functions.

- ➢ In section 13.1, you learned how to use various formatting styles
- ➢ In section 13.2, you learned how to format output using ToString output.

Chapter 14

Formatting Date and Time

❖ Learning how to Format Date and Time

14.1 Formatting Date and Time Using Predefined Formats

Very often, we need to format date and time in a Vb2010 program. You can format date and time using predefined formats and user-defined formats. The predefined formats of date and time are shown in Table 14.1

Format	Explanation
Format (Now, "General date")	Formats the current date and time
Format (Now, "Long Date")	Displays the current date in long format
Format (Now, "Short date")	Displays current date in short format
Format (Now, "Long Time")	Display the current time in long format
Format (Now, "Short Time")	Display the current time in short format

Table 14.1 Predefined formats of date and time

* Instead of "General date", you can also use the abbreviated format "G", i.e. Format (Now, "G"). You can use the abbreviated format "T" for "Long Time" and the abbreviated format "t" for "short time".

Example 14.1

```
Private Sub Button1_Click(ByVal sender As System.Object, ByVal e As
System.EventArgs) Handles Button1.Click

        Label1.Text = Format(Now, "General Date")
        Label2.Text = Format(Now, "Long Date")
        Label3.Text = Format(Now, "short Date")
        Label4.Text = Format(Now, "Long Time")
        Label5.Text = Format(Now, "Short Time")

End Sub
```

Date and time in different formats are shown in the Figure 14.1 .

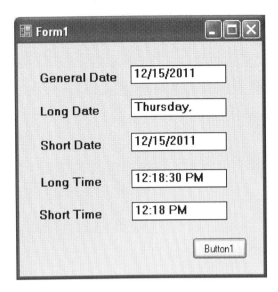

Figure 14.1: Time in different Format

14.2 Formatting Date and Time Using User-Defined formats

Besides using the predefined formats, you can also use the user-defined formatting functions. The general format of a user-defined date and time is

Format (expression, style)

Format	Explanation
Format (Now, "M")	Displays current month and date
Format (Now, "MM")	Displays current month in double digits
Format (Now, "MMM")	Displays abbreviated name of the current month
Format (Now, "MMMM")	Displays full name of the current month.
Format (Now, "dd/MM/yyyy")	Displays current date in the day/month/year format
Format (Now, "MMM,d,yyyy")	Displays current date in the Month, Day, Year Format
Format (Now, "h:mm:ss tt")	Displays current time in hour:minute:second format and show am/pm
Format (Now, "MM/dd/yyyy h:mm:ss)	Displays current date and time in hour:minute:second format

Table 14.2: some of the user-defined format functions for date and time

Example 14.2

Private Sub Button1_Click(ByVal sender As System.Object, ByVal e As System.EventArgs) Handles Button1.Click, Button2.Click, Button3.Click

```
Label1.Text = Format(Now, "M")
Label2.Text = Format(Now, "MM")
Label3.Text = Format(Now, "MMM")
Label4.Text = Format(Now, "MMMM")
Label5.Text = Format(Now, "dd/MM/yyyy")
Label6.Text = Format(Now, "MMM,d,yyyy")
Label7.Text = Format(Now, "h:mm:ss tt")
Label8.Text = Format(Now, "MM/dd/yyyy h:mm:ss tt")
```

End Sub

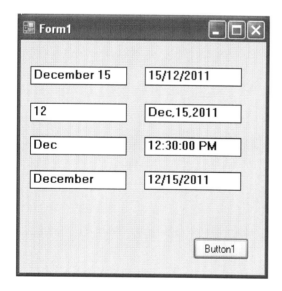

Figure 14.2: Date and Time in different formats

14.3 Formatting Date and Time Using ToString Method

Another way to format date and time is to use the ToString method. ToString is used together with the standard date and time format specifiers.

For example, to format present date of the current culture in the computer that by default is using the US system, we can use the syntax

Now.ToString ("d")

It displays the date as short date in the form of **mm/dd/yy**

For other culture, you have to include the culture code. You can refer to the culture code in Appendix II. For example, Malaysia culture code is ms-MY, the time format is **dd/mm/yy**, similar to the French culture code. The syntax to include the culture code is as follows:

Now.ToString ("d", CultureInfo.CreateSpecificCulture ("ms-MY"))

Some of the standard date and time format specifiers are listed in Table 14.3

Format specifier	Description	Examples
"d"	Displays date in the short date pattern such as mm/dd/yy.	Now.ToString ('d') displays the date in the mm/dd/yy format. Now.ToString("d", CultureInfo.CreateSpecificCulture("fr-FR")) displays the date in dd/mm/yy format
"D"	Displays date in the Long date pattern.	Now.ToString("D") displays the date as Monday, November 07, 2011 Now.ToString("D", CultureInfo.CreateSpecificCulture("fr-FR"))

		displays the date as mardi 7 novembre 2011
"f"	Displays full date/time pattern (short time). .	Now.ToString("f") displays the date/time as Tuesday, November 07, 2011 12:08 Now.ToString("f", CultureInfo.CreateSpecificCulture("fr-FR")) Displays the date time as mardi 7 novembre 2011 00:08
"F"	Displays full date/time pattern (long time).	Now.ToString("F") displays the date/time as Tuesday, November 8, 2011 12:08:30 AM Now.ToString("F", CultureInfo.CreateSpecificCulture("fr-FR")) displays the date time as mardi 8 novembre 2011 00:15:31
"g"	Displays general date /time pattern (short time).	Now.ToString("g") displays the date/time as 11/08/2011 12:08 AM Now.ToString("g", CultureInfo.CreateSpecificCulture("fr-FR")) displays the date time as 08/11/2011 00:08
"G"	Displays general date /time pattern (long time). .	Now.ToString("G") displays date/time as 11/08/2011 12:08:30 AM Now.ToString("G", CultureInfo.CreateSpecificCulture("fr-FR")) displays the date time as 08/11/2011 00:08:30

"M", "m"	Displays month /day pattern.	Now.ToString ("M") displays month/day as November 08 Now.ToString("M", CultureInfo.CreateSpecificCulture("fr-FR")) displays month/day as 8 novembre
"t"	Display short time pattern. .	Now.ToString ("t") displays time as 12.08AM Now.ToString("t", CultureInfo.CreateSpecificCulture("fr-FR")) displays time as 00.08
"T"	Displays long time pattern. .	Now.ToString ("T") displays time as 12.08:30 AM Now.ToString("T", CultureInfo.CreateSpecificCulture("fr-FR")) displays time as 00.08:30
"Y", "y"	Displays year / month pattern.	Now.ToString ("Y") displays year/month as November, 2011 Now.ToString("Y", CultureInfo.CreateSpecificCulture("fr-FR")) displays year/month as novembre 2011

Table 14.3: standard date and time format specifiers

Summary

You learned how to format date and time in this chapter.

> ➤ In Section 14.1, you learned how to format date and time using predefined format.

> ➤ In Section 14.2, you learned how to format date and time using user-defined format.

> ➤ In section 14.2, you learned how to format date and time using ToString method.

Chapter 15

Creating User-Defined Functions

❖ Learning how to create user-defined function

Function is a method that returns a value to the calling procedure. You can create user-defined function to perform certain calculations and some other tasks.

The general format of a function is as follows:

Public Function functionName **(param As dataType,..........) As dataType**

or

Private Function functionName **(param As dataType,..........) As dataType**

* Public indicates that the function is applicable to the whole project and

* Private indicates that the function is only applicable to a certain module or procedure.

* param is the argument or parameter of the function that can store a value. You can specify more than one parameter, separated by commas.

Example 15.1: Cube Root Calculator

In this example, we will create a program that calculates the cube root of a number. The function code is

```
Public Function cubeRoot(ByVal myNumber As Single) As Single
    Return myNumber ^ (1 / 3)
  End Function
```

The keyword *Return* is to compute the cube root and return the value to the calling procedure.

Place the function procedure in the general section of the module.

Next, design an interface and create a procedure that call the function and display the value to user. To create the interface, place three label controls and one textbox into the form. Rename the label to be LblCubeRoot.and use it to display the cube root

Now click on the textbox and enter the following code:

```
Private Sub TextBox1_TextChanged(ByVal sender As System.Object, ByVal e As
System.EventArgs) Handles TextBox1.TextChanged

        LblCubeRoot.Text = cubeRoot(Val(TextBox1.Text))

End Sub
```

Press F5 to run the program and you should get the following output:

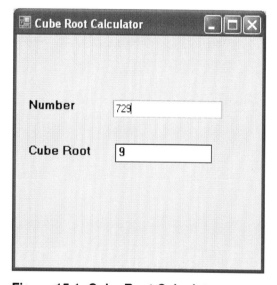

Figure 15.1: Cube Root Calculator

Example 15.2

In this example, we create a function that can convert mark to grade, a handy function to manage college examinations or tests processing. In this function, we use the Select case control structure to convert marks of different range to different grades.

```
Public Function grade(ByVal mark As Single) As String
    Select Case mark
        Case Is > 100
            Return "Invalid mark"
        Case Is >= 80
            Return "A"
        Case Is >= 70
            Return "B"
        Case Is >= 60
            Return "C"
        Case Is >= 50
            Return "D"
        Case Is >= 40
            Return "E"
        Case Is >= 0
            Return "F"
        Case Is < 0
            Return "Invalid mark"

    End Select
    End Function
```

We need to design an interface for the user to enter the marks and we need to write a procedure to call the function and display the grade on a label. To achieve the purpose, we will insert the following controls and set their properties as follows:

Control	Properties
Label1	Text: Mark ; font bold
Label2	Text:Grade ; font bold
TextBox1	Name: TxtMark
Lable3	LblGrade

Table 15.1

We also need to write a procedure to call the function. Click on Textbox1 and enter the following code:

```
Private Sub TxtMark_TextChanged(ByVal sender As System.Object, ByVal e As System.EventArgs) Handles TxtMark.TextChanged

    If TxtMark.Text = "" Then
       Lbl_Grade.Text = "Enter Mark"
    Else
       Lbl_Grade.Text = grade(Val(TxtMark.Text))
    End If

End Sub
```

The procedure will compute the value entered in the textbox by the user by calling the grade () function and display the result on the label Lbl_Grade.

The output is shown in Figure 15.2:

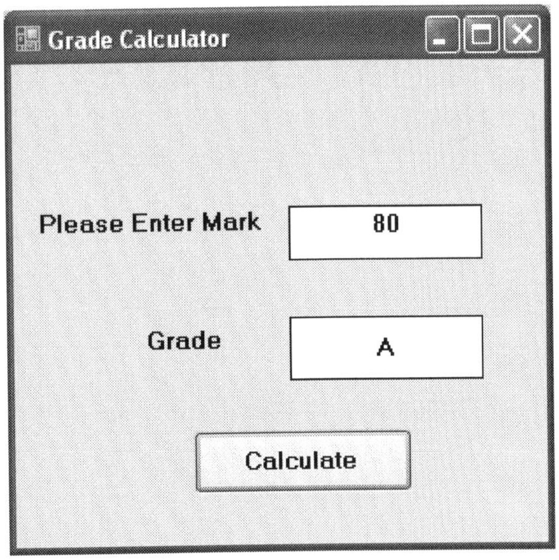

Figure 15.2

Example 15.3: BMI calculator

Many people are obese now and it could affect their health seriously. If your BMI is more than 30, you are obese. You can refer to the following range of BMI values for your weight status.

Underweight = <18.5

Normal weight = 18.5-24.9

Overweight = 25-29.9

Obesity = BMI of 30 or greater

Now we shall create a calculator in Vb2010 that can calculate the body mass index, or BMI of a person based on the body weight in kilogram and the body height in meter. BMI can be calculated using the formula   weight/ (height) ^{2}, where weight is measured in kg and height in meter. If you only know your weight and height in lb and feet, then you need to convert them to the metric system. To build the calculator, we need to create a function that contains two parameters, namely height and weight, as follows:

Public Function BMI (ByVal height, ByVal weight)

Return Val ((weight) / (height ^ 2))

End Function

Next, design an interface that includes four labels, three of them is used for labeling height, weight and BMI and the last one is to display the value of BMI. We also inserted two text boxes to accept input of height and weight from the user. Lastly, insert a button for the user to click on in order to start the calculation process. Set the properties as follows:

Control	Properties
Label1	Text : Height (in meter) Font : Microsoft Sans Serif, 10 pt, style=Bold
Label2	Text : Weight (in kg) Font : Microsoft Sans Serif, 10 pt, style=Bold
Label3	Text : BMI Font : Microsoft Sans Serif, 10 pt, style=Bold
Label4	Name: LblBMI Text : Blank Font : Microsoft Sans Serif, 10 pt, style=Bold
Textbox1	Name; TxtH Text : Blank Font : Microsoft Sans Serif, 10 pt, style=Bold
Textbox2	Name; TxtW Text : Blank Font : Microsoft Sans Serif, 10 pt, style=Bold

Now, click on the button and enter the following code:

LblBMI.Text = Format (BMI(TxtH.Text, TxtW.Text), "0.00")

We use the format function to configure the output value to two decimal places. This procedure will call the function BMI to perform calculation based on the values input by the user using the formula defined in the function.

The output is shown in Figure 15.3

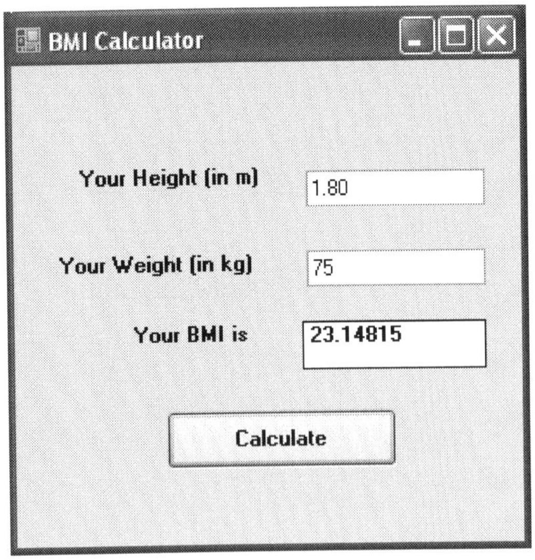

Figure 15.3

Example 15.4: Future Value Calculator

In this example, the user can calculate the future value of a certain amount of money he has today based on the interest rate and the number of years from now, supposing he or she will invest this amount of money somewhere .The calculation is based on the compound interest rate. This reflects the time value of money.

Future value is calculated based on the following formula:

$$PV = FV\left(1 + \frac{i}{100}\right)^n$$

The function to calculate the future value involves three parameters namely the present value (PV), the interest rate (i) and the length of period (n). The function code is shown below:

```
Public Function FV(ByVal PV As Single, ByVal i As Single, ByVal n As Integer) As
Double

    Return PV * (1 + i / 100) ^ n

End Function
```

The code to display the Future Value is

```
Private Sub BtnCal_Click(ByVal sender As System.Object, ByVal e As
System.EventArgs) Handles BtnCal.Click

    LblFV.Text = FV(TxtPV.Text, TxtI.Text, TxtYear.Text).ToString("C")

End Sub
```

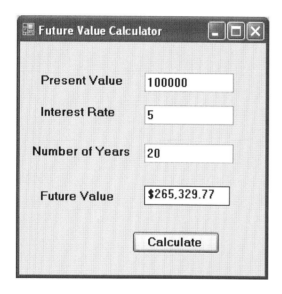

Figure 15.4: The Future Value Calculator

Summary

In this chapter, you learned how to create user-defined functions. Among them are the cube root calculator, the examination grades calculator, the BMI calculator and the future value calculator.

Chapter 16

Using Advanced Controls

❖ Learn how to use the Check Box

❖ Learn how to use the Radio Button

❖ Learn how to use List Box

❖ Learn how to use Combo Box

16.1 The Check Box

The Check box is a very useful control in Visual Basic 2010. It allows the user to select one or more items by checking the checkbox or checkboxes concerned. For example, in the Font dialog box of any Microsoft Text editor like FrontPage, there are many checkboxes under the Effects section such as that shown in the diagram below.

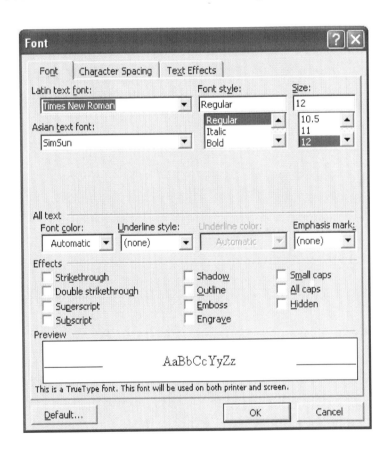

Figure 16.1: Microsoft Font Dialog Box

In Visual Basic 2010, you may create a shopping cart that allows the user to click on checkboxes that correspond to the items they intend to purchase, and calculates the total payment at the same time. The code is shown in Example 16.1 below.

Example 16.1: Shopping Cart

```
Private Sub BtnCalculate_Click(ByVal sender As System.Object, ByVal e As
System.EventArgs) Handles BtnCalculate.Click
Const LX As Integer = 100
Const BN As Integer = 500
Const SD As Integer = 200
Const HD As Integer = 80
Const HM As Integer = 300
Const AM As Integer = 160
Dim sum As Integer


If CheckBox1.Checked = True Then
sum += LX
End If


If CheckBox2.Checked = True Then
sum += BN
End If


If CheckBox3.Checked = True Then
sum += SD
End If
```

```
If CheckBox4.Checked = True Then

sum += HD

End If

If CheckBox5.Checked = True Then

sum += HM

End If


If CheckBox6.Checked = True Then

sum += AM

End If

Label5.Text = sum.ToString("c")
```

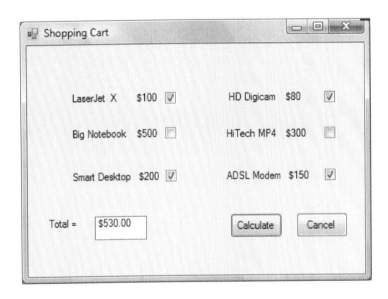

Figure 16.2: The Shopping Cart

Here is another example

Example 16.2

```
Private Sub Button1_Click(ByVal sender As System.Object, ByVal e As
System.EventArgs) Handles Button1.Click

        Const large As Integer = 10.0
        Const medium As Integer = 8
        Const small As Integer = 5
        Dim sum As Integer
        If CheckBox1.Checked = True Then

            sum += large

        End If

        If CheckBox2.Checked = True Then

            sum += medium

        End If

        If CheckBox3.Checked = True Then

            sum += small

        End If


        Label5.Text = sum.ToString("c")
```

Example 16.3

In this example, the user can enter text into a textbox and format the font using the three checkboxes that represent bold, italic and underline.

The code is as follow:

```
Private Sub CheckBox1_CheckedChanged(ByVal sender As System.Object,
ByVal e As System.EventArgs) Handles CheckBox1.CheckedChanged

If CheckBox1.Checked Then

        TextBox1.Font = New Font(TextBox1.Font, TextBox1.Font.Style Or
        FontStyle.Bold)
        Else
        TextBox1.Font = New Font(TextBox1.Font, TextBox1.Font.Style And Not
        FontStyle.Bold)

End If
End Sub


Private Sub CheckBox2_CheckedChanged(ByVal sender As System.Object,
ByVal e As System.EventArgs) Handles CheckBox2.CheckedChanged
If CheckBox2.Checked Then

        TextBox1.Font = New Font(TextBox1.Font, TextBox1.Font.Style Or
        FontStyle.Italic)
        Else
        TextBox1.Font = New Font(TextBox1.Font, TextBox1.Font.Style And Not
        FontStyle.Italic)
```

```
End If

End Sub


Private Sub CheckBox3_CheckedChanged(ByVal sender As System.Object,

ByVal e As System.EventArgs) Handles CheckBox3.CheckedChanged

If CheckBox3.Checked Then


    TextBox1.Font = New Font(TextBox1.Font, TextBox1.Font.Style Or

    FontStyle.Underline)

    Else

    TextBox1.Font = New Font(TextBox1.Font, TextBox1.Font.Style And Not

    FontStyle.Underline)


End If

End Sub
```

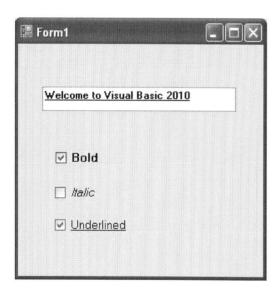

Figure 16.3

- The above program uses the CheckedChanged event to respond to the user selection by checking a particular checkbox; it is similar to the click event.

The statement

TextBox1.Font = New Font(TextBox1.Font, TextBox1.Font.Style Or FontStyle.Italic)

retains the original font type but change it to italic font style.

TextBox1.Font = New Font(TextBox1.Font, TextBox1.Font.Style And Not FontStyle.Italic)

will also retain the original font type but change it to regular font style. (The other statements employ the same logic)

16.2 The Radio Button

The radio button is also a very useful control in Visual Basic 2010. However, it operates differently from the check boxes. While the checkboxes work independently and allows the user to select one or more items, radio buttons are mutually exclusive, which means the user can only choose one item only out of a number of choices. Here is an example that allows the users to select one color only.

Example 16.4

The Code:

```
Dim strColor As String

Private Sub RadioButton8_CheckedChanged(ByVal sender As System.Object, ByVal e
As System.EventArgs) Handles RadioButton8.CheckedChanged

    strColor = "Red"

End Sub

Private Sub RadioButton7_CheckedChanged(ByVal sender As System.Object, ByVal e
As System.EventArgs) Handles RadioButton7.CheckedChanged

    strColor = "Green"
```

End Sub

Private Sub RadioYellow_CheckedChanged(ByVal sender As System.Object, ByVal e As System.EventArgs) Handles RadioYellow.CheckedChanged

    strColor = "Yellow"

End Sub

Private Sub Button1_Click(ByVal sender As System.Object, ByVal e As System.EventArgs) Handles Button1.Click

    Label2.Text = strColor

End Sub

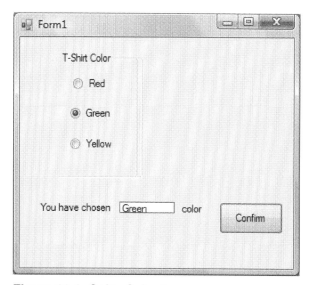

Figure 16.4: Color Selection

Although the user may only select one item at a time, he may make more than one selection if those items belong to different categories. For example, the user wish to choose T-shirt size and color, he needs to select one color and one size, which means one selection in each category. This is done using the Groupbox control under the containers categories. After inserting the Groupbox into the form, you can proceed to insert the radio buttons into the Groupbox. Only the radio buttons inside the Groupbox are mutually exclusive, they are not mutually exclusive with the radio buttons outside the Groupbox. In Example 16.5, the users can select one color and one size of the T-shirt.

Example 16.5

```
Dim strColor As String
Dim strSize As String

Private Sub RadioButton8_CheckedChanged(ByVal sender As System.Object, ByVal e
As System.EventArgs) Handles RadioButton8.CheckedChanged

        strColor = "Red"

End Sub
Private Sub RadioButton7_CheckedChanged(ByVal sender As System.Object, ByVal e
As System.EventArgs) Handles RadioButton7.CheckedChanged
        strColor = "Green"
End Sub

Private Sub RadioYellow_CheckedChanged(ByVal sender As System.Object, ByVal e

As System.EventArgs) Handles RadioYellow.CheckedChanged

        strColor = "Yellow"

End Sub


Private Sub Button1_Click(ByVal sender As System.Object, ByVal e As

System.EventArgs) Handles Button1.Click

        Label2.Text = strColor

        Label4.Text = strSize

End Sub
```

```
Private Sub RadioXL_CheckedChanged(ByVal sender As System.Object, ByVal e As
System.EventArgs) Handles RadioXL.CheckedChanged
        strSize = "XL"
End Sub


 Private Sub RadioL_CheckedChanged(ByVal sender As System.Object, ByVal e As
System.EventArgs) Handles RadioL.CheckedChanged
        strSize = "L"
 End Sub



Private Sub RadioM_CheckedChanged(ByVal sender As System.Object, ByVal e As
System.EventArgs) Handles RadioM.CheckedChanged
        strSize = "M"
 End Sub


 Private Sub RadioS_CheckedChanged(ByVal sender As System.Object, ByVal e As
System.EventArgs) Handles RadioS.CheckedChanged
        strSize = "S"
 End Sub
```

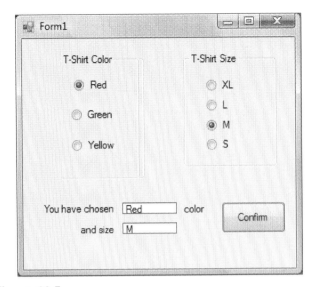

Figure 16.5

16.3 The List Box

A list box is an object that displays a list of items. You can populate the list box with items at design time or at runtime. You can also remove the items from the list box. You can also clear an item from the list box based on its index, starting from 0.To demonstrate the usage of the List Box, start a new project and name it as myListBox. Change the Form1 text to Name List. Insert a list box into the form and change its name to myNameList in the properties window. Next, add two buttons to Form1, name the first one as BtnAdd and change the text to Add Name. Name the second one as BtnRemove and change its text to Remove Name.

16.3.1 Adding Items to the List Box at Design Time

To add items to a list box, go to the properties window of the ListBox and scroll to find the Items property. On the left of the Items property, you can see the word **Collection** with a three-dot button on the right as shown in Figure 16.6

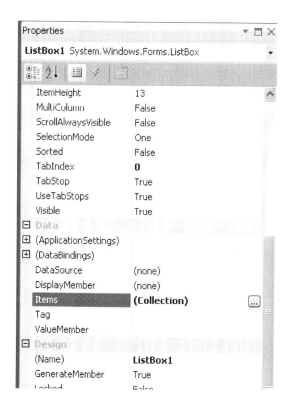

Figure 16.6

Now click on the three-dot button to go into the String Collection Editor. In the String Collection Editor, you can add items to the list, one item per line. Here, we add a list of ten names, as shown in Figure 16.7.

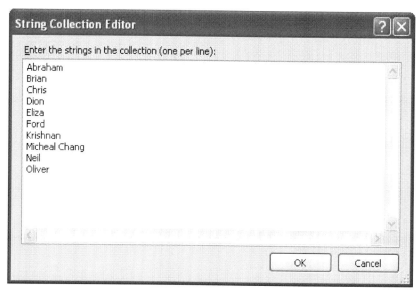

Figure 16.7

Press F5 to run the program and you can see the list of names entered earlier by clicking the drop-down arrow of the combo box, as shown in Figure 16.8

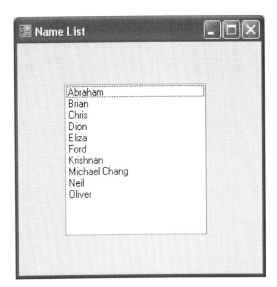

Figure 16.8

16.3.2 Adding Items to the List Box at Run Time

To add an item to the List Box at runtime, use the following code:

```
Listbox.Items.Add("Name")
```

In our example, you can add the name Wigan using the following statement.

```
myNameList.Items.Add("Wigan")
```

When you run the program and click the add name button, the name Wigan will be added to the end of the list.

You can also let the user add items to the combo box via an input box. Place the following code under the BtnAdd_Click procedure.

```
Dim userMsg As String

userMsg = Microsoft.VisualBasic.InputBox("Enter a name and Click OK",

"Names Entry Form", "Enter name here", 100, 200)

myNameList.Items.Add(userMsg)
```

When you run the program and click the Add Name button, the input box as shown in Figure 16.9 will pop out. You can then enter a name and click the OK button, the name Hugo will be added to the list.

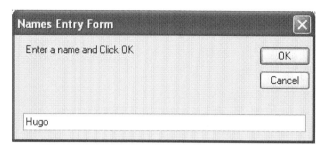

Figure 16.9

To return the index of a particular item, you can use the keyword IndexOf. Referring to our previous example, if you wish to find out the index of a certain name such as "Dion", you can use the syntax as shown below:

    myNameList.Items.IndexOf("Dion")

It will return a value of 3 as it is the fourth item.

To get the index of the selected item, you can use the following syntax:

    myNameList.SelectedIndex

16.3.3 Removing and Clearing Items from the List Box

To remove items from the list in the combo box, we use the **Remove ( )** method
The syntax using our example is:

    ListBox.Items.Remove("ItemName")

Referring to our example, you can remove the name Dion using the following statement:

    myNamelist.Items.Remove("Dion")

To remove an item according to its index, we need to use the RemoveAt( ) method. The Syntax is:

ListBox.Items.RemoveAt("Index")

Referring to our previous example, we can remove the second name using the following syntax:

myNamelist.Items.RemoveAt(1)

To remove a selected item, we can use the following syntax:

If NameList.SelectedIndex <> -1 Then

   myNameList.Items.RemoveAt(NameList.SelectedIndex)

End if

16.4 The Combo Box

Combo box is a kind of list box but it does not display all the items at one time. Instead, it displays one item at a time and provides a drop-down list where the user and click and view the other items. The advantage of using a combo box is that it saves space. As in the list box, you can add or remove items in the combo box at design time or at run time. You can also clear all the items from the combo box. Every item in a list box is identified by an index, starting from 0.

16.4.1 Adding Items to the Combo Box at Design Time

To demonstrate adding items at design time, start a project and name it MyComboBox. Change the caption of Form1 to A Collection of Names. Now, add a combo box by dragging the ComboBox control to the form. Change the name of the ComboBox to NameList . Next, add two buttons to the form name the first one as BtnAdd and change the text to Add Name. Name the second one as BtnRemove and change its text to Remove

Name. Now, go to the properties window of the ComboBox and scroll to find the Items property. On the left of the Items property, you can see the word **Collection** with a three-dot button on the right as shown in Figure 16.10

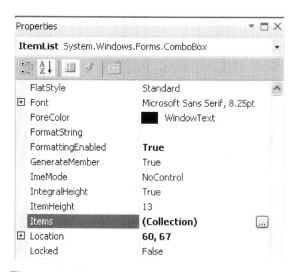

Figure 16.10

Now click on the three-dot button to go into the String Collection Editor. In the String Collection Editor, you can add items to the list, one item per line. Here, we add a list of ten names, as shown in Figure 16.11

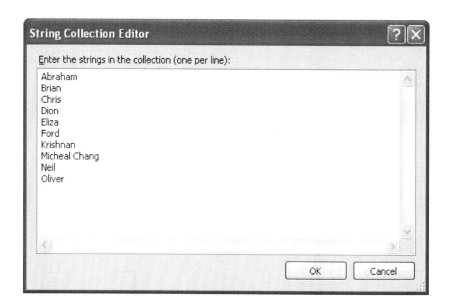

Figure 16.11

Press F5 to run the program and you can see the list of names entered earlier by clicking the drop-down arrow of the combo box, as shown in Figure 16.12

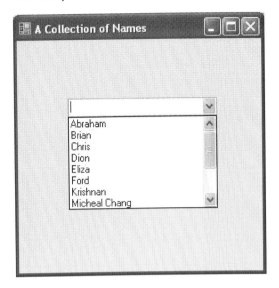

Figure 16.12

16.4.2 Adding Items to the Combo Box at Runtime

To add item to the combo box at runtime, we use the following syntax:

ComboBox1. Items.Add(ItemName)

In our example, the code to add names to the list is:

NameList.Items.Add(name)

For example, we can add the name **Robert** using the following code

NameList.Items.Add("Robert")

You can also let the user add items to the combo box via an input box. The code is shown below:

Private Sub BtnAdd_Click(ByVal sender As System.Object, ByVal e As

System.EventArgs) Handles BtnAdd.Click

```
    Dim userMsg As String

    userMsg = Microsoft.VisualBasic.InputBox("Enter a name and Click

    OK", "Names Entry Form", "Enter name here", 100, 200)

    NameList.Items.Add(userMsg)

  End Sub
```

When the user clicks the Add Name button, a dialog with an empty box will appear so that he or she can fill in the name, as shown below. Once he or she enter a name and click OK, the name will appear in the combo box list.

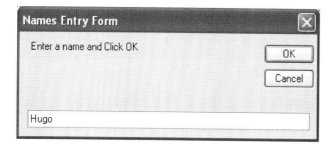

Figure 16.13

To return the index of a particular item, you can use the keyword IndexOf. Referring to our previous example, if you wish to find out the index of a certain name such as "Dion", you can use the syntax as shown below:

```
    NameList.Items.IndexOf("Dion")
```

It will return a value of 3 as it is the fourth item.

To get the index of the selected item, you can use the following syntax:

```
    NameList.SelectedIndex
```

16.4.3: Removing Items from the list in the Combo Box

To remove items from the list in the combo box, we use the **Remove ( )** method

The syntax using our example is:

ComboBox.Items.Remove("ItemName")

Referring to our example, you can remove the name Dion using the following statement:

Namelist.Items.Remove("Dion")

To remove an item according to its index, we need to use the RemoveAt( ) method.
The Syntax is:

ComboBox.Items.RemoveAt("Index")

Referring to our previous example, we can remove the second name using the following syntax:

Namelist.Items.RemoveAt(1)

To remove a selected item, we can use the following syntax:

If NameList.SelectedIndex <> -1 Then

NameList.Items.RemoveAt(NameList.SelectedIndex)

End If

Summary
In this chapter, you learned how to write code for four advanced controls, namely the check box, the radio button, the list box and the combo box. You also learned how to add items to the list box and the combo box.

Chapter 17

Creating a Simple Web Browser

❖ Learning how to create a simple web browser

Since the advent of the Internet and the World Wide Web, almost everyone is surfing the Internet for information. In addition, when we are talking Internet surfing, it refers to using a program to browse the World Wide Web; this type of program is known as a browser. At the beginning of the Internet age, we have the primitive Internet browsing program called Gopher where you can only see text contents. However, the then famous Netscape Navigator soon replaced it. Moreover, Microsoft created the Internet explorer, a default browser that shipped with newer versions of Windows.

Today, basically everyone navigates the Internet using commercially produced web browsers such the Internet Explorer produced by Microsoft or those open source browsers designed by the experts such Mozilla FireFox , Opera and the latest Chrome created by Google. However, is it cool if we can create our very own web browser that we can customize to our own taste and design? Yes, you can do that in VB2010, and rather easy too. In this chapter, we will show you how to create a simple web browser and get it running in a few minutes.

First, start a new project in VB2010 and name it with any name that you like. Here I am using the name VB2010 Webbrowser. Change the name of Form1 to VB2010 Webbrowser and the text property to My First Web Browser and set its size property to 640,480. Next, you need to add a control so that your web browser can connect to the Internet, and this very engine is called the WebBrowser control, located in the Toolbox on the left side, set its size property to 600,400. Next, drag a text box and place it at the bottom of the WebBrowser control, this will be the address bar where the user can enter the URL. Lastly, place a command button beside the text box and label it as Go. The design interface is shown in Figure 17.1 below:

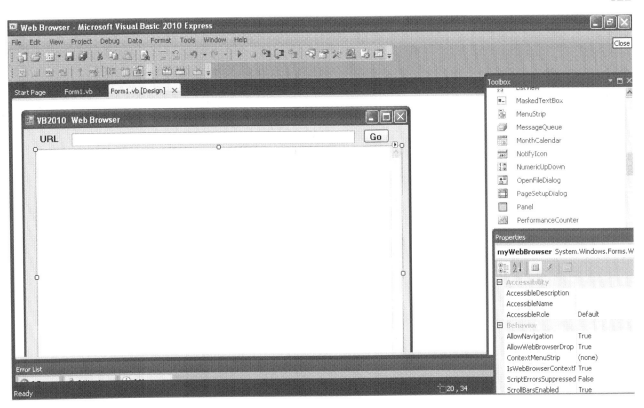

Figure 17.1: Web Browser

The Code

The code for the web browser is surprisingly simple; it is only a single line code! Double click on the Go button and key in the following code:

```
Public Class

Private Sub Button1_Click ByVal sender As System.Object, ByVal   As
System.EventArgs) Handles Button1.Click

    myWebBrowser.Navigate (TextBox1.Text)

End Sub

End Class
```

Now run the program, type in any URL and click the Go button. You will be able to browse any web page you want.

123

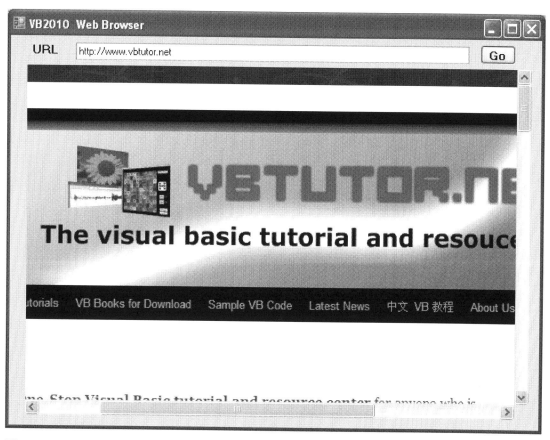

Figure 17.2

Summary

In this chapter, you learned how to create a simple web browser and a more advanced web browser.

Chapter 18

Errors Handling

❖ Learning how to handle errors

18.1 Introduction

Error handling is an essential procedure in Visual Basic 2010 programming because it can help make the program error-free. An error-free program can run smoothly and efficiently, and the user does not have to face all sorts of problems such as program crash or system hang.

Errors often occur due to incorrect input from the user. For example, the user might make the mistake of attempting to enter a text (string) to a box that is designed to handle only numeric values such as the weight of a person, the computer will not be able to perform arithmetic calculation for text therefore will create an error. We call these errors synchronous errors.

Therefore, a good programmer should be more alert to the parts of program that could trigger errors and should write errors handling code to help the user in managing the errors. Writing errors handling code is a good practice for Visual Basic programmers, so do not try to finish a program fast by omitting the errors handling code. However, there should not be too many errors handling code in the program as it create problems for the programmer to maintain and troubleshoot the program later.

VB2010 has improved a lot in built-in errors handling compared to Visual Basic 6. For example, when the user attempts to divide a number by zero, Vb2010 will not return an error message but gives the 'infinity' as the answer (although this is mathematically incorrect, because it should be undefined)

18.2 Using On Error GoTo Syntax

Visual Basic 2010 still supports the VB6 errors handling syntax that is the On Error GoTo program_label structure. Although it has a more advanced error handling method, we shall deal with that later. We shall now learn how to write errors handling code in VB2010. The syntax for errors handling is

On Error GoTo   program_label

Where **program_label** is the section of code that is designed by the programmer to handle the error committed by the user. Once the program detects an error, the program will jump to the program_label section for error handling.

Example 18.1: Division by Zero

In this example, we will deal with the error of entering non-numeric data into the textboxes that suppose to hold numeric values. The program_label here is error_hanldler. When the user enter a non-numeric values into the textboxes, the error message will display the text "One of the entries is not a number! Try again!" If no error occurs, it will display the correct answer. Try it out yourself.

The Code

```
Public Class Form1

Private Sub CmdCalculate_Click(ByVal sender As System.Object, ByVal e As
System.EventArgs) Handles CmdCalculate.Click

        Lbl_ErrorMsg.Visible = False

        Dim firstNum, secondNum As Double

        On Error GoTo error_handler

        firstNum = Txt_FirstNumber.Text
```

secondNum = Txt_SecondNumber.Text

Lbl_Answer.Text = firstNum / secondNum

Exit Sub 'To prevent error handling even the inputs are valid

error_handler:

Lbl_Answer.Text = "Error"

Lbl_ErrorMsg.Visible = True

Lbl_ErrorMsg.Text = " One of the entries is not a number! Try again!"

End Sub

End Class

The Output is shown in Figure 18.1

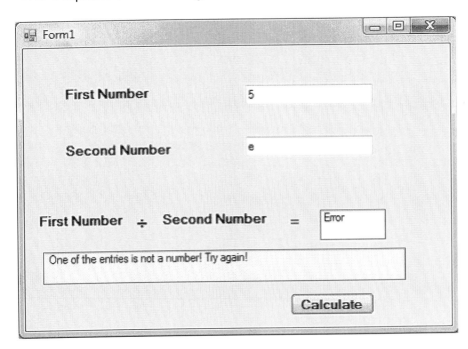

Figure 18.1

18.3 Errors Handling using Try...Catch...End Try   Structure

VB2010 has adopted a new approach in handling errors, or rather exceptions handling. It is supposed to be more efficient than the old On Error Goto method, where it can handles various types of errors within the Try...Catch...End Try structure.

The structure looks like this

```
Try

    statements

Catch exception_variable as Exception

    statements to deal with exceptions

End Try
```

Example 18.2

This is a modification of Example 18.1. Instead of using On Error GoTo method, we use the Try...Catch...End Try method. In this example, the Catch statement will catch the exception when the user **enters** a non-numeric data and return the error message. If there is no exception, there will not any action from the Catch statement and the program returns the correct answer.

The code

```
Private Sub CmdCalculate_Click(ByVal sender As System.Object, ByVal e As System.EventArgs) Handles CmdCalculate.Click

    Lbl_ErrorMsg.Visible = False

    Dim firstNum, secondNum, answer As Double

    Try

    firstNum = Txt_FirstNumber.Text
```

```
        secondNum = Txt_SecondNumber.Text

        answer = firstNum / secondNum

        Lbl_Answer.Text = answer

        Catch ex As Exception

        Lbl_Answer.Text = "Error"

        Lbl_ErrorMsg.Visible = True

        Lbl_ErrorMsg.Text" One of the entries is not a number! Try again!"

        End Try

End Sub
```

The output is shown in Figure 18.2

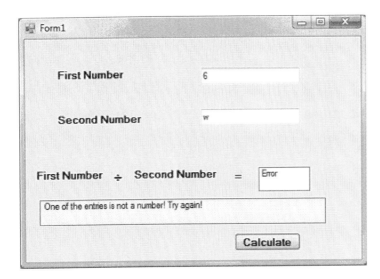

Figure 18.2

Summary
- ➤ In section 18.1, you learned the basic principle of handling errors.
- ➤ In section 18.2, you learned how to use On Error Goto Syntax.
- ➤ In section 18.3, you learned how to use Try...Catch...End Try structure.

Chapter 19

Reading and Writing Files

❖ Learning how to create program to read and write text files

19.1 Introduction

To be able to open a file and read the data from storage unit of a computer, such as a hard drive as well as able to save the data into the storage unit are important functions of a computer program. In fact, the ability to store, retrieve and modify data makes a computer a powerful tool in database management.

In this Chapter, we will learn how to manage data that is stored as a text file. Using text file is an easy way to manage data, although it is not as sophisticated as full-fledged database management software such as SQL Server, Microsoft Access and Oracle. Visual Basic 2010 allows the user to create a text file, save the text file as well as read the text file. It is relatively easy to write code for the above purposes in VB2010.

Reading and writing to a text file in VB2010 required the use of the StreamReader class and the StreamWriter class respectively. StreamReader is a tool that enables the streaming of data by moving it from one location to another so that the user can read it. For example, it allows the user to read a text file that is stored in a hard drive. On the other hand, the StreamWriter class is a tool that can write data input by the user to a storage device such as the hard drive.

19.2 Reading a Text File

In order to read a file from the hard disk or any storage device, we need to use the StreamReader class. To achieve that, first we need to include the following statement in the program code:

```
Imports System.IO
```

This line has to precede the whole program code, as it is higher in hierarchy than the StreamReader Class. In Fact, this is the concept of object oriented programming where StreamReader is part of the namespace System.IO. You have to put it on top of the whole program (i.e. above the Public Class Form 1 statement). The word import means we import the namesapce System.IO into the program. Once we have done that, we can declare a variable of the streamReader data type with the following statement:

Dim FileReader As StreamReader

If we do not include the Imports System.IO, we have to use the statement

Dim FileReader As IO.StreamReader

each time we want to use the StreamReader class.

Now, start a new project and name it in whatever name you wish, we named it TxtEditor here. Now, insert the OpenFileDialog control into the form because we will use it to read the file from the storage device. The default name of the OpenFileDialog control is OpenFileDialog1, you can use this name or you can rename it with a more meaningful name. The OpenFileDialog control will return a DialogResult value that can determine whether the user clicks the OK button or Cancel button. We will also insert a command button and change its displayed text to 'Open'. The user can use it to open and read a certain text file. The following statement will accomplish the task above.

```
Dim results As DialogResult
results = OpenFileDialog1.ShowDialog
If results = DialogResult.OK Then
'Code to be executed if OK button was clicked
Else
'Code to be executed if Cancel button was clicked
End If
```

Next, we insert a textbox ,name it TxtEditor and set its Multiline property to true. It is used for displaying the text from a text file. We also insert a button and name it BtnOpen. In order to read the text file, we need to create a new instant of the streamReader and connect it to a text file with the following statement:

FileReader = New StreamReader(OpenFileDialog1.FileName)

In addition, we need to use the ReadToEnd method to read the entire text of a text file and display it in the text box. The syntax is:

TxtEditor.Text = FileReader.ReadToEnd( )

Lastly, we need to close the file by using the Close() method. The entire code is shown in the box below:

The Code

```
Imports System.IO
Public Class Form1
Private Sub BtnOpen_Click(ByVal sender As System.Object, ByVal e As
System.EventArgs) Handles BtnOpen.Click
    Dim FileReader As StreamReader
    Dim results As DialogResult
    results = OpenFileDialog1.ShowDialog
    If results = DialogResult.OK Then
    FileReader = New StreamReader(OpenFileDialog1.FileName)
    TxtEditor.Text = FileReader.ReadToEnd()
    FileReader.Close()
    End If
End Sub
```

The Design Interface is shown in Figure 19.1

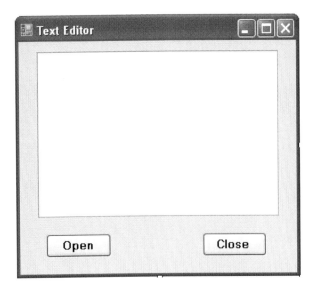

Figure 19.1

The Open Dialog box is shown in Figure 19.2

Figure 19.2

The Output Interface is shown in Figure 19.3

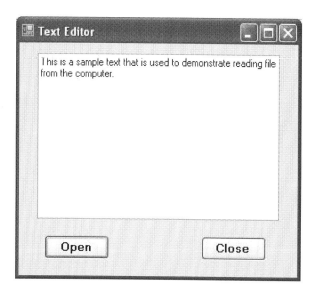

This is a sample text that is used to demonstrate reading file from the computer.

Figure 19.3

19.3 Writing to a Text File

Writing a text file means storing the text entered by the user via the textbox into a storage device such as a hard drive. It also means saving the file. To accomplish this task, we need to deploy the StreamWriter Class. You also need to insert the SaveFileDialog control into the form as it is used to save the data into the storage unit like a hard drive. The default name for the SaveFileDialog control is SaveFileDialog1. We also insert another button and name it as BtnSave. The Code is the same as the code for reading the file, you just change the StreamReader to StreamWriter, and the method from ReadToEnd to Write. The code is shown below:

The code

```
Imports System.IO
Public Class Form1
Private Sub BtnSave_Click(ByVal sender As System.Object, ByVal e As
System.EventArgs)
        Dim FileWriter As StreamWriter
```

```
        Dim results As DialogResult

        results = SaveFileDialog1.ShowDialog

        If results = DialogResult.OK Then

        FileWriter = New StreamWriter(SaveFileDialog1.FileName, False)

        FileWriter.Write(TxtEditor.Text)

        FileWriter.Close()

        End If

   End Sub
```

The Output Interface is shown in Figure 19.4

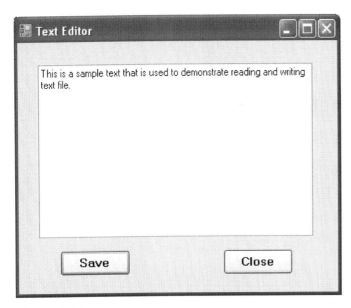

Figure 19.4

When you click the save button, the program will prompt you to key in a file name and the text will be save as a text file. Finally, you can combine the two programs together and create a text editor that can read and write text file, as shown in the Figure 19.5 below.

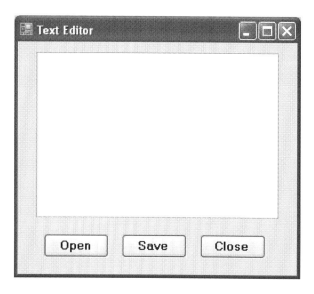

Figure 19.5

Summary

In this chapter, you learned how to create program to read and write files

➢ In section 19.1, you learned the basic principle of handling reading and saving data to storage unit of a computer.

➢ In section 19.2, you learned how to write code to read text file. You learned how to import the namespace System.IO and include the streamReader class in your code.

➢ In section 19.3, you learned how to design program to write text file to the storage unit of the computer. You learned how to include StreamWriter class in your code so that your program can write file to the computer.

Chapter 20

Creating and Managing Graphics

❖ Learning how to create and manage graphics

20.1 Introduction

Creating and managing graphics is easy in earlier versions of Visual Basic as they have built-in drawing tools. For example, In Visual Basic 6, the drawing tools are included in the toolbox where the programmer just need to drag the shape controls into the form to create rectangle, square, ellipse, circle and more. However, its simplicity has the shortcomings; you do not have many choices in creating customized drawings.

Since Visual Basic evolved into a fully OOP language under the VB.net framework, shape controls are no longer available. Now the programmer needs to write code to create various shapes and drawings. Even though the learning curve is steeper, the programmer can write powerful code to create all kinds of graphics. You can even design your own controls

VB2010 offers various graphics capabilities that enable programmers to write code that can draw all kinds of shapes and even fonts. In this Chapter, you will learn how to write code to draw lines and shapes on the VB interface.

20.2 Creating the Graphics Object

Before you can draw anything on a form, you need to create the Graphics object in vb2008. A graphics object is created using a CreateGraphics() method. You can create a graphics object that draw to the form itself or a control. For example, if you wish to draw to the form, you can use the following statement:

```
Dim myGraphics As Graphics =me.CreateGraphics
```

If you want the graphics object to draw to a picturebox, you can write the following statement:

```
Dim myGraphics As Graphics = PictureBox1.CreateGraphics
```

You can also use the textbox as a drawing surface, the statement is:

```
Dim myGraphics As Graphics = TextBox1.CreateGraphics
```

The Graphics object that is created does not draw anything on the screen until you call the methods of the Graphics object. In addition, you need to create the **Pen** object as the drawing tool. We will examine the code that can create a pen in the following section.

20.3 Creating the Pen object

The **Pen** object can be created using the following code:

```
myPen = New Pen(Brushes.DarkMagenta, 10)
```

In the code, myPen is a Pen variable. You can use any variable name instead of myPen. The first argument of the pen object defines the color of the drawing line and the second argument defines the width of the drawing line.

You can also create a Pen using the following statement:

```
Dim myPen As Pen
```

```
myPen = New Pen(Drawing.Color.Blue, 5)
```

Where the first argument defines the color (*here is blue, you can change that to red or whatever color you want*) and the second argument defines the width of the drawing line.

Having created the Graphics and the Pen object, you are now ready to draw graphics on the screen, which we will show you in the following section.

20.4 Drawing a Line

In this section, we will show you how to draw a straight line on the Form. First, launch Visual basic 2008 Express. In the startup page, drag a button into the form. Double click on the button and key in the following code.

```
Private Sub Button1_Click(ByVal sender As System.Object, ByVal e As
System.EventArgs) Handles Button1.Click

    Dim myGraphics As Graphics = me.CreateGraphics

    Dim myPen As Pen

    myPen = New Pen(Brushes.DarkMagenta, 10)

    myGraphics.DrawLine(myPen, 10, 10, 100, 10)

End Sub
```

The second line created the Graphics object and the third and fourth line create the Pen object. The fifth line draws a line on the Form using the DrawLine method. The first argument uses the Pen object created by you, the second argument and the third arguments define the coordinate of the starting point of the line, the fourth and the last arguments define the ending coordinate of the line. The general syntax to draw line is object.DrawLine(Pen, x1, y1, x2, y2)

Run the program and you can a see purple line appear on the screen, as shown in Figure 20.1.

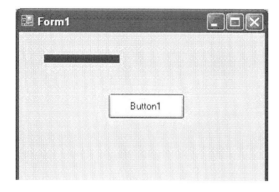

Figure 20.1

20.5 Creating a Rectangle

To draw a rectangle on the screen in VB2010, there are two ways:

(i)The first way is to draw a rectangle directly using the **DrawRectangle** method by specifying its upper-left corner's coordinates and its width and height. You also need to create a Graphics and a Pen object to handle the actual drawing. The method to draw the rectangle is **DrawRectangle**.

The syntax is:

myGrapphics.DrawRectangle (myPen, X, Y, width, height)

Where myGraphics is the variable name of the Graphics object and myPen is the variable name of the Pen object created by you. You can use any valid and meaningful variable names. X, Y is the coordinate of the upper left corner of the rectangle while width and height are self-explanatory, i.e., the width and height of the rectangle.

The sample code is shown below:

```
Dim myPen As Pen
myPen = New Pen(Drawing.Color.Blue, 5)
Dim myGraphics As Graphics = Me.CreateGraphics
myGraphics.DrawRectangle (myPen, 0, 0, 100, 50)
```

(ii) The second way is to create a rectangle object first and then draw this triangle using the **DrawRectangle** method. The syntax is as shown below:

myGraphics.DrawRectangle (myPen, myRectangle)

Where **myRectangle** is the rectangle object created by you, the user.

The code to create a rectangle object is as shown below:

```
Dim myRectangle As New Rectangle

myRect.X = 10

myRect.Y = 10

myRect.Width = 100

myRect.Height = 50
```

You can also create a rectangle object using a one-line code as follows:

```
Dim myRectangle As New Rectangle(X, Y, width, height)
```

The code to draw the above rectangle is

```
myGraphics.DrawRectangle (myPen, myRectangle)
```

The sample code is shown below:

```
Private Sub Button1_Click(ByVal sender As System.Object, ByVal e As System.EventArgs) Handles Button1.Click

    Dim myRect As New Rectangle

    myRect.X = 10

    myRect.Y = 10

    myRect.Width = 100

    myRect.Height = 50
```

```
        Dim myPen As Pen

        myPen = New Pen(Drawing.Color.Blue, 5)

        Dim myGraphics As Graphics = Me.CreateGraphics

        myGraphics.DrawRectangle(myPen, myRect)

    End Sub
```

20.6 Customizing Line Style of the Pen Object

The shapes we draw so far were drawn with solid line, we can customize the line style of the Pen object so that we have dotted line, line consisting of dashes and more. For example, the syntax to draw with dotted line is shown below:

```
        myPen.DashStyle=Drawing.Drawing2D.DashStyle.Dot
```

The last argument, Dot, specifies a particular line DashStyle value, a line that makes up of dots. The following code draws a rectangle with red dotted line.

```
Private Sub Button1_Click(ByVal sender As System.Object, ByVal e As
System.EventArgs) Handles Button1.Click
        Dim myPen As Pen
        myPen = New Pen(Drawing.Color.Red, 5)
        Dim myGraphics As Graphics = Me.CreateGraphics
        myPen.DashStyle = Drawing.Drawing2D.DashStyle.Dot
        myGraphics.DrawRectangle(myPen, 10, 10, 100, 50)
End Sub
```

Run the program and you can see a dotted-line rectangle appears on the screen, as shown in Figure 20.2.

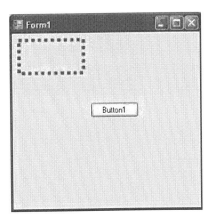

Figure 20.2

20.7 Drawing an Ellipse

First, we need to understand the principal behind drawing an ellipse. The basic structure of any shape is a rectangle. Ellipse is an oval shape that is bounded by a rectangle, as shown in Figure 20.3 below:

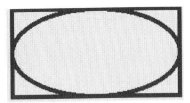

Figure 20.3

Therefore, you need to create a Rectangle object before you can draw an ellipse. This rectangle serves as a bounding rectangle for the ellipse. On the other hand, you can still draw an ellipse with the **DrawEllipse** method without first creating a rectangle. We will show you both ways.

In the first method, let say you have created a rectangle object known as myRectangle and a pen object as myPen, then you can draw an ellipse using the following statement:

myGraphics.DrawEllipse (myPen, myRectangle)

* Assume you have also already created the Graphics object myGraphics.

The following is an example of the full code.

```
Dim myPen As Pen

myPen = New Pen(Drawing.Color.Blue, 5)

Dim myGraphics As Graphics = Me.CreateGraphics

Dim myRectangle As New Rectangle

myRectangle.X = 10

myRectangle.Y = 10

myRectangle.Width = 200

myRectangle.Height = 100

myGraphics.DrawEllipse (myPen, myRectangle)
```

Run the program and you see the ellipse appears on the screen, as shown in Figure 20.4.

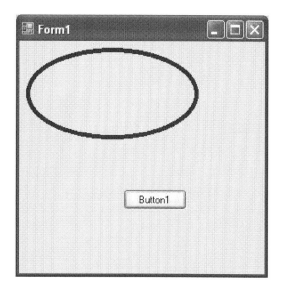

Figure 20.4

The second method is using the DrawEllipse method without creating a rectangle object. Off course, you still have to create the Graphics and the Pen objects. The syntax is:

```
myGraphics.DrawEllipse(myPen, X,Y, Width, Height)
```

Where (X, Y) are the coordinates of the upper left corner of the bounding rectangle, width is the width of the ellipse and height is the height of the ellipse.

The following is an example of the full code:

```
Dim myPen As Pen

myPen = New Pen(Drawing.Color.Blue, 5)

Dim myGraphics As Graphics = Me.CreateGraphics

myGraphics.DrawEllipse (myPen, 10, 10, 200, 100)
```

20.8 Drawing a Circle

After you have learned how to draw an ellipse, drawing a circle becomes very simple. We use exactly the same methods used in the preceding section but modify the width and height so that they are of the same values.

The following examples draw the same circle.

Example (a)

```
Dim myPen As Pen

myPen = New Pen(Drawing.Color.Blue, 5)

Dim myGraphics As Graphics = Me.CreateGraphics

Dim myRectangle As New Rectangle

myRectangle.X = 10

myRectangle.Y = 10

myRectangle.Width = 100

myRectangle.Height = 100

myGraphics.DrawEllipse(myPen, myRectangle)
```

Example (b)

```
Dim myPen As Pen

myPen = New Pen(Drawing.Color.Blue, 5)

Dim myGraphics As Graphics = Me.CreateGraphics

myGraphics.DrawEllipse(myPen, 10, 10, 100, 100)
```

Run the program and you can see a circle appears on the screen, as shown in Figure 20.5

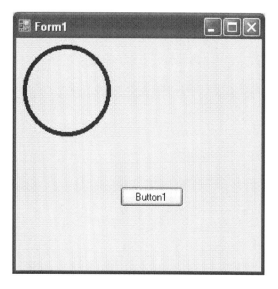

Figure 20.5

20.9 Drawing Text

In order to draw text on the screen, we can use the DrawString method. The format is as follows:

```
myGraphics.DrawString (myText, myFont, mybrush, X , Y)
```

Where myGraphics is the Graphics object, myText is the text you wish to display on the screen, myFont is the font object created by you, myBrush is the brush style created by you and X, Y are the coordinates of upper left corner of the Text.

You can create your **Font object** using the following statement:

```
myFont = New System.Drawing.Font("Verdana", 20)
```

Where the first argument of the font is the font typeface and the second argument is the font size. You can add a third argument as font style, either bold, italic, underline.

Here are some examples:

```
myFont = New System.Drawing.Font("Verdana", 20, FontStyle.Bold)
myFont = New System.Drawing.Font("Verdana", 20, FontStyle.Underline)
myFont = New System.Drawing.Font("Verdana", 20, FontStyle.Italic)
myFont = New System.Drawing.Font("Verdana", 20, FontStyle.Regular)
```

To create the **Brush** object, you can use the following statement:

```
Dim myBrush As Brush
myBrush = New Drawing.SolidBrush(Color.BrushColor)
```

Besides the seven colors, some of the common Brush Colors are AliceBlue, AquaMarine Beige, DarkMagenta, DrarkOliveGreen, SkyBlue and more. You do not have to remember the names of all the colors, the intelliSense will let you browse through the colors in a drop-down menu once you type the dot after the word Color.

Now we shall proceed to draw the font using the sample code below:

```
Dim myGraphics As Graphics = Me.CreateGraphics
Dim myFont As Font
Dim myBrush As Brush
myBrush = New Drawing.SolidBrush(Color.DarkOrchid)
```

```
myFont = New System.Drawing.Font("Verdana", 20, FontStyle.Underline)
myGraphics.DrawString("Visual Basic 2010", myFont, myBrush, 10, 10)
```

Run the program above and you can see the text "Visual Basic 2010 "appears on the screen, as shown in Figure 20.6.

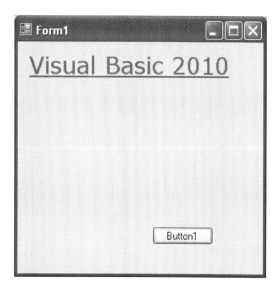

Figure 20.6

You can modify the preceding code if you do not want to create the Font and the Brush objects. You can use the font of an existing object such as the Form and the System Colors. Replace the last line in the preceding example with this line.

```
myGraphics.DrawString("Visual Basic 2010", me.Font,
System.Drawing.Brushes.DarkOrchid, 10, 10)
```

You can also add an InputBox, which let the user enter his or her message then displays the message on the screen.

This is the sample code is as follows:

```
Dim myGraphics As Graphics = Me.CreateGraphics
Dim myFont As Font
Dim myBrush As Brush
Dim userMsg As String
```

```
UserMsg = InputBox("What is your message?", "Message Entry Form", "Enter
your message here", 100, 200)

myBrush = New Drawing.SolidBrush(Color.DarkOrchid)

myFont = New System.Drawing.Font("Verdana", 20, FontStyle.Underline)

myGraphics.DrawString (userMsg, myFont, myBrush, 10, 10)
```

20.10 Drawing a Polygon

Polygon is a closed plane figure bounded by three or more straight sides. In order to draw a polygon on the screen, we need to define the coordinates of all the points (also known as vertices) that joined up to form the polygon.

The syntax to define the points of a polygon with vertices A_1, A_2 ...A_n as follows:

```
Dim A1 As New Point(X1,Y1)
Dim A2 As New Point(X2,Y2)
        .
Dim An as New Point(Xn,Yn)
```

After declaring the points, we need to define a point structure that group all the points together using the following syntax:

```
Dim myPoints As Point() = {A1, A2, A3,.....,An}
```

Finally, create the graphics object and use the DrawPolygon method to draw the polygon using the following syntax:

```
Dim myGraphics As Graphics = Me.CreateGraphics
myGraphics.DrawPolygon(myPen, myPoints)
```

Where myPen is the Pen object created using the following syntax:

```
myPen = New Pen(Drawing.Color.Blue, 5)
```

Example : Drawing a Triangle

A triangle is a polygon with three vertices. Here is the sample code:

```
Dim myPen As Pen

Dim A As New Point(10, 10)

Dim B As New Point(100, 50)

Dim C As New Point(60, 150)

Dim myPoints As Point() = {A, B, C}

myPen = New Pen(Drawing.Color.Blue, 5)

Dim myGraphics As Graphics = Me.CreateGraphics

myGraphics.DrawPolygon (myPen, myPoints)
```

Run the program and you should see a triangle appears on the screen, as shown in Figure 20.7.

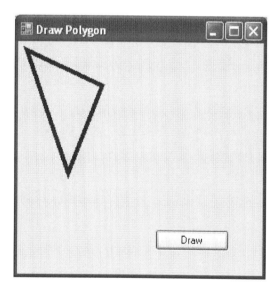

Figure 20.7

Example: Drawing a Quadrilateral

A quadrilateral is a polygon consists of four sides, so you need to define four vertices. The following is the code:

```
Dim myPen As Pen

Dim A As New Point(10, 10)

Dim B As New Point(100, 50)

Dim C As New Point(120, 150)

Dim D As New Point(60, 200)

Dim myPoints As Point() = {A, B, C, D}

myPen = New Pen(Drawing.Color.Blue, 5)

Dim myGraphics As Graphics = Me.CreateGraphics

myGraphics.DrawPolygon (myPen, myPoints)
```

Run the program and you can see a polygon appears on the screen, as shown in Figure 20.8.

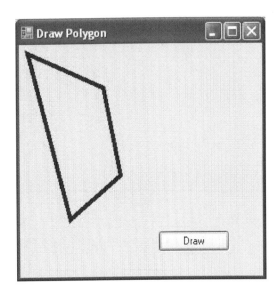

Figure 20.8

20.11: Drawing a Pie

In order to draw a pie, you can use the DrawPie method of the graphics object. As usual, you need to create the Graphics and the Pen objects. The syntax for drawing a pie is:

myGraphics.DrawPie (myPen, X, Y, width, height, StartAngle, SweepAngle)

Where X and Y are the coordinates of the bounding rectangle, other arguments are self-explanatory. Both StartAngle and SweepAngle are measured in degree. SweepAngle can take possible or negative values. If the value is positive, it sweep through clockwise direction while negative means it sweep through anticlockwise direction.

Example: Draw a pie that starts with 0 degree and sweep clockwise through 60 degree.

Dim myPen As Pen

myPen = New Pen(Drawing.Color.Blue, 5)

Dim myGraphics As Graphics = Me.CreateGraphics

myGraphics.DrawPie(myPen, 50,50, 150,150,0,60)

Run the program and you can see a pie appears on the screen, as shown in Figure 20.9

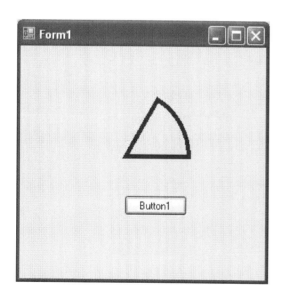

Figure 20.9

In previous sections, we have learned how to draw rectangle, ellipse, circle, polygon and pie with outlines only. In this section, we will show you how to fill the shapes with color, or simply solid shapes. You can use the following three methods to fill the shapes; they are **FillRectangle, FillEllipse, FillPolygon** and **FillPie**.

To fill the above shapes with color, create the Brush object using the following syntax:

    myBrush = New SolidBrush(Color.myColor)

myColor should be replaces by the names of the colors such as red, blue, yellow and more. You do not have to worry about the names of the colors because the intellisense will display the colors and enter the period after the Color key word.

```
Dim myPen As Pen
Dim myBrush As Brush
Dim myGraphics As Graphics = Me.CreateGraphics
myPen = New Pen(Drawing.Color.Blue, 5)
myBrush = New SolidBrush(Color.Coral)
myGraphics.DrawRectangle (myPen, 0, 0, 150, 150)
myGraphics.FillRectangle (myBrush, 0, 0, 150, 150)
```

This program draws a coral color square, as shown in Figure 20.10.

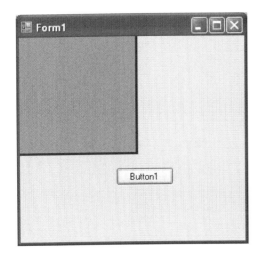

Figure 20.10

20.12 Drawing and Filling an Ellipse

The syntax to fill an ellipse with the color defined by the brush object is:

```
myGraphics.FillEllipse (myBrush, 0, 0, 150, 150)
```

The complete code is shown in the example below:

```
Dim myPen As Pen

Dim myBrush As Brush

Dim myGraphics As Graphics = Me.CreateGraphics

myPen = New Pen(Drawing.Color.Blue, 5)

myBrush = New SolidBrush(Color.Coral)

myGraphics.DrawEllipse(myPen, 0, 0, 150, 150)

myGraphics.Ellipse(myBrush, 0, 0, 150, 150)
```

Run the program and you can see a coral color ellipse appears on the screen, as shown in Figure 20.11

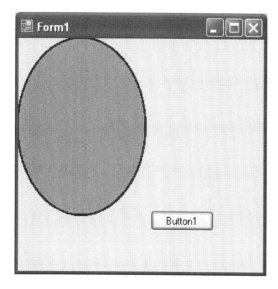

Figure 20.11

20.13 Drawing and Filling a Polygon

The syntax to fill a polygon with the color defined by the brush object is:

```
myGraphics.FillPolygon (myBrush, myPoints)
```

The complete code is shown in the example below:

```
Dim myPen As Pen
Dim myBrush As Brush
Dim A As New Point(10, 10)
Dim B As New Point(100, 50)
Dim C As New Point(120, 150)
Dim D As New Point(60, 200)
Dim myPoints As Point() = {A, B, C, D}
myPen = New Pen(Drawing.Color.Blue, 5)
myBrush = New SolidBrush(Color.Coral)
Dim myGraphics As Graphics = Me.CreateGraphics
myGraphics.DrawPolygon(myPen, myPoints)
myGraphics.FillPolygon(myBrush, myPoints)
```

Running the code produces the image as shown in Figure 20.12.

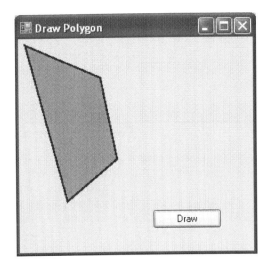

Figure 20.12

20.14 Drawing and Filling a Pie

The syntax to fill a pie with the color defined by the brush object is:

myGraphics.FillPie(myBrush, X, Y, width, height, StartAngle, SweepAngle)

The complete code is shown in the example below:

Dim myPen As Pen

Dim myBrush As Brush

myPen = New Pen(Drawing.Color.Blue, 5)

myBrush = New SolidBrush(Color.Coral)

Dim myGraphics As Graphics = Me.CreateGraphics

myGraphics.DrawPie(myPen, 30, 40, 150, 150, 0, 60)

myGraphics.FillPie(myBrush, 30, 40, 150, 150, 0, 60)

Run the program and you can see a coral color pie appears on the screen, as shown in Figure 20.13.

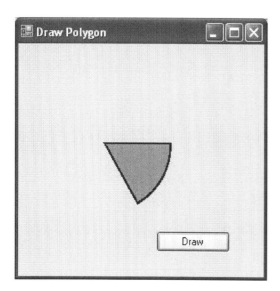

Figure 20.13

Summary

In this chapter, you learned how to draw various shapes and fill them with color.

➢ In section 20.1, you learned the basic concepts about graphics creation in VB2010.

➢ In section 20.2, you learned how to use the CreateGraphics() method to create a graphics object.

➢ In section 20.3, you learned how to create the Pen object

➢ In section 20.4, you learned how to use the DrawLine method to draw a line.

➢ In section 20.5, you learned how to use the DrawRectangle method to create a rectangle.

➢ In section 20.6, you learned how to customize the line style of the Pen object.

➢ In section 20.7, you learned how to use the DrawEllipse method to draw an ellipse.

➢ In section 20.8, you learned how to use the DrawEllipse method to draw a circle

➢ In section 20.9, you learned how to use the DrawString method to draw text on the screen.

➢ In section 20.10, you learned how to use the DrawPolygon method to draw a polygon.

➢ In section 20.11, you learned how to use the DrawPie method to draw a pie.

➢ In section 20.12, you learned how to fill an ellipse with color.

➢ In section 20.13, you learned how to fill a polygon with color.

➢ In section 20.14, you learned how to fill a pie with color.

Chapter 21

Arrays

❖ Learning how to create arrays in VB2010

21.1 Introduction to Arrays

By definition, an array is a list of variables with the same data type and name. When we work with a single item, we only need to use one variable. However, if we have a list of items, which are of similar type to deal with, we need to declare an array of variables instead of using a variable for each item

For example, if we need to enter one hundred names, it is difficulty to declare 100 different names; this is a waste of time and efforts. Therefore, instead of declaring one hundred different variables, we need to declare only one array. We differentiate each item in the array by using subscript, the index value of each item, for example name(0), name(1),name(2) ....etc. , which will make declaring variables streamline and much systematic.

21.2 Dimension of an Array

An array can be one dimensional or multidimensional. One-dimensional array is like a list of items or a table that consists of one row of items or one column of items. Table 21.1 shows a one-dimensional array.

Student Name	Name(0)	Name(1)	Name(2)	Name(3)	Name(4)	Name(5)

Table 21.1 One-dimensional Array

A two dimensional array is a table of items that make up of rows and columns. The format for a one-dimensional array is ArrayName(x), the format for a two dimensional array is ArrayName(x, y) and a three dimensional array is ArrayName(x, y, z). Normally it is sufficient to use one-dimensional and two-dimensional arrays; you only need to use higher dimensional arrays if you need to deal with problems that are more complex.

21.3 Declaring an Array

We can use Public or Dim statement to declare an array just as the way we declare a single variable. The Public statement declares an array so that it can be used throughout the entire application while the Dim statement declares an array that can be used only in a local procedure.

21.3.1 Declaring One Dimensional Array

The general format to declare a one-dimensional array is as follow:

Dim arrayName(subs) as dataType

The argument subs indicates the last subscript in the array.

Example 21.1

Dim CusName(9) as String

declare an array that consists of 10 elements starting from CusName(0) to CusName(9).

Example 21.2

Dim Count (100 to 500) as Integer

The statement above declares an array that consists of the first element starting from Count (100) and ends at Count (500)

Example 21.3: Creating a Name List

In this program, we want let the user create a name list by entering name into a list box. At runtime, the user will be prompted to enter ten student names. The names entered will appear in a list box. First, start a new project and name it Student Data. Next, insert a list box and a button into the form. Change properties of the controls as follows:

Control	Properties
Form1	Name: StudentList Text: Student List
ListBox	Name: NameList
Control1	Name: BtnAdd Text: Add Name

Table 21.3

Next, click the button and key in the following code:

```
Private Sub BtnAdd_Click(ByVal sender As System.Object, ByVal e As
System.EventArgs) Handles BtnAdd.Click
    Dim studentName(9) As String
    Dim num As Integer
    For num = 0 To 9
        studentName(num) = Microsoft.VisualBasic.InputBox("Enter a name and
        Click OK", "Names Entry Form", "Enter name here", 100, 200)
        NameList.Items.Add(studentName(num))
    Next

    End Sub
```

When you press F5 and run the program, you will see a popup dialog box where you can enter a name. After you have entered the name and click Ok, the same dialog box will appear again for you to enter the second student name. The process will repeat ten times. The dialog box is as shown in Figure 21.1

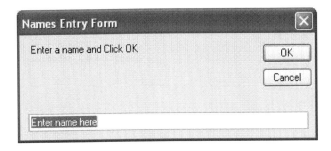

Figure 21.1

After entering ten names, you can see the ten names appear on the list box, as shown in Figure 21.2

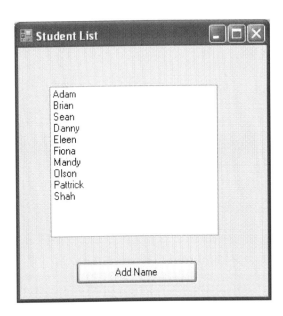

Figure 21.2

21.3.1 Declaring Two Dimensional Array

The general format to declare a two dimensional array is as follow:

Dim ArrayName(Sub1,Sub2) as dataType

Total number of elements will be (sub1+1)x(sub2+1). For example,

Dim Score(2,3) will produce an array that comprises 3x4=12 elements, as shown in Table 21.2

Score(0,0)	Score(0,1)	Score(0,2)	Score(0,3)
Score(1,0)	Score(1,1)	Score(1,2)	Score(1,3)
Score(2,0)	Score(2,1)	Score(2,2)	Score(2,3)

Table 21.2 Two Dimensional Array

Example 21.4: Managing Students' Examination Scores

In this example, we want to key in the examination marks for five students and four subjects. Since we are handling two variables here, i.e. name and subject, we need to declare a two dimensional array, as follows:

Dim score (4, 3) as String

The first dimension represents student names and the second dimension represents the subjects. Combining both produces the scores for each student for each subject. For example, the score for the first student for the first subject will be score (0, 0). We can design a program to let the user enter the student names, subject titles as well as the scores. We need to use two nested loops involving the For...Next structure. The first loop gets the students' names and the second loop gets the students' scores for the four subjects. To achieve the purpose, we introduce a one-dimensional array StudentName(4) to store the names of the five students. We also introduce a one dimensional array mark(3) to store the mark of every subject for every student .After entering the name of the first student and his scores, we get something like this:

Adam   45   60   56   80

The scores of students in array form are shown in Table 21.3

| studentName(0)=Adam | Score(0,0)=45 | Score(0,1)=60 | Score(0,2)=56 | Score(0,3)=80 |

Table 21.3; Scores for first students

The variable mark are assigned the values of the scores as shown in table 21.4

| studentName(0)=Adam | mark(0)=45 | mark(1)=60 | mark(2)=56 | mark(3)=80 |

Table 21.4: Score in terms of mark

The process repeats until the user has entered all the data. The completed data appear as a two-dimensional array, as shown in terms of scores in Table 21.5 and in terms of marks in Table 21.6.

studentName(0)=Adam	score(0,0)=45	score(0,1)=56	score(0,2)=78	score(0,3)=68
studentName(1)=Brian	score(1,0)=64	score(1,1)=76	score(1,2)=80	score(1,3)=90
studentName(2)=Florence	score(2,0)=87	score(2,1)=80	score(2,2)=90	score(2,3)=100
studentName(3)=Gloria	score(3,0)=45	score(3,1)=54	score(3,2)=34	score(3,3)=48
studentName(4)=Mandy	score(4,0)=56	score(4,1)=87	score(4,2)=68	score(4,3)=66

Table 21.5

studentName(0)=Adam	mark(0)=45	mark(1)=56	mark(2)=78	mark(3)=68
studentName(1)=Brian	mark(0)=64	mark(1)=76	mark(2)=80	mark(3)=90
studentName(2)=Florence	mark(0)=87	mark(1)=80	mark(2)=90	mark(3)=100
studentName(3)=Gloria	mark(0)=45	mark(1)=54	mark(2)=34	mark(3)=48
studentName(4)=Mandy	mark(0)=56	mark(1)=87	mark(2)=68	mark(3)=66

Table 21.6

In this program, we insert a list box and name it NameList. We also introduce a button and name it BtnAdd. Change the form title from Form1 to "Examination Scores"

Now click the button and enter the code. In the code, we declare studentName (4) and mark(3) as one-dimensional array

The code

```
Private Sub BtnAdd_Click(ByVal sender As System.Object, ByVal e As
System.EventArgs) Handles BtnAdd.Click
  Dim studentName(4) As String
    Dim score(4, 3) As String
    Dim mark(3) As String
    Dim num1, num2 As Integer
    For num1 = 0 To 4
      studentName(num1) = Microsoft.VisualBasic.InputBox("Enter a name and
      Click OK", "Names Entry Form", "Enter name here", 100, 200)


      For num2 = 0 To 3
        score(num1, num2) = Microsoft.VisualBasic.InputBox("Enter score and
        Click OK", "Scores Entry Form", "Enter Score here", 100, 200)
        mark(num2) = score(num1, num2)
      Next
      NameList.Items.Add(studentName(num1) & vbTab & mark(0) & vbTab &
      mark(1) & vbTab & mark(2) & vbTab & mark(3))


    Next
  End Sub

Private Sub Form1_Load(ByVal sender As Object, ByVal e As System.EventArgs)
Handles Me.Load
    'To Label the subjects' titles at the top of the list
    NameList.Items.Add("" & vbTab & "English" & vbTab & "Sience" & vbTab &
```

```
        "Math" & vbTab & "Art")

    'To draw a separation line between the subjects' titles and the scores

    NameList.Items.Add("" & vbTab & "-----------------------------------------------
        -----------")

End Sub
```

The examination scores are shown in Figure 21.3

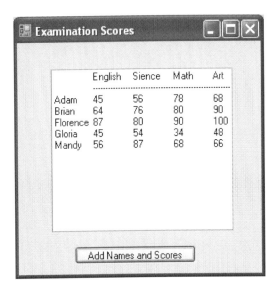

Figure 21.3

The above example has demonstrated the practical usage of arrays. If you wish to add more features to the program, you can modify the code easily, like writing the code to obtain the total mark and average mark.

Summary
  ➢ In this section 21.1, you learned that an array is a list of variables with the same data type and name
  ➢ In section 21.2, you learned about arrays of different dimensions.
  ➢ In section 21.3, you learned how to declare arrays of different dimensions.

Chapter 22

Using Timer

❖ Learning how to Use Timer in VB2010

In this chapter, we shall show you how to use timer in VB2010. You use Timer is to control and manage events that are time related. For example, you need timer to create a clock, a stopwatch, a dice, animation and more.

22.1 Creating a Clock

To create a clock, you need to use the Timer control that comes with Visual Basic 2010 Express. The Timer control is a control object that is only used by the developer, it is invisible during runtime and it does not allow the user to interact with it.

To create the clock, first start a new project in Visual Basic 2010 Express and select a new Windows Application. You can give the project any name you wish, but we named it MyClock. Change the caption of Form1 to MyClock in the properties window. Now add the Timer control to the form by dragging it from the ToolBox. Next, insert a label control into the form. Change the Font size of the label to 14 or any size you wish, and set the Font alignment to be middle center. Before we forget, you shall also set the Interval property of the Timer control to 1000, which reflects a one second interval (1unit= 1 millisecond). Now, you are ready for the coding. It is only a simple one-line code, that is:

```
Label1.Text = TimeOfDay
```

To create the clock, click on the Timer control and insert the following code

```
Private Sub Timer1_Tick(ByVal sender As System.Object, ByVal e As
System.EventArgs) Handles Timer1.Tick

    Label1.Text = TimeOfDay

End Sub
```

The image of the digital clock is shown in Figure 22.1

Figure 22.1

You can also use the code **Now.ToString( )** to show the time as well as date, that is:

The full code is

```
Private Sub Timer1_Tick(ByVal sender As System.Object, ByVal e As
System.EventArgs) Handles Timer1.Tick

    Label1.Text = Now.ToString

End Sub
```

The Clock is shown in Figure 22.2

Figure 22.2

22.2 Creating a Stopwatch

We can create a simple stopwatch using the Timer control. Start a new project and name it stopwatch. Change the Form1 caption to Stopwatch. Insert the Timer control into the form and set its interval to 1000, which is equal to one second. Also, set the timer Enabled property to False so that it will not start ticking when the program starts. Insert three command buttons and change their names to StartBtn, StopBtn and ResetBtn respectively. Change their text to "Start", "Stop" and "Reset" accordingly. Now enter the code as follows:

```
Private Sub Timer1_Tick(ByVal sender As System.Object, ByVal e As
System.EventArgs) Handles Timer1.Tick

        'To increase one unit per second

        Label1.Text = Val(Label1.Text) + 1

End Sub




Private Sub StopBtn_Click(ByVal sender As System.Object, ByVal e As
System.EventArgs) Handles StopBtn.Click

'To stop the Timer
    Timer1.Enabled = False
End Sub
Private Sub StartBtn_Click(ByVal sender As System.Object, ByVal e As
System.EventArgs) Handles StartBtn.Click
        'To start the Timer
        Timer1.Enabled = True
End Sub
```

Private Sub ResetBtn_Click(ByVal sender As System.Object, ByVal e As System.EventArgs) Handles ResetBtn.Click

  'To reset the Timer to 0

  Label1.Text = 0

End Sub

The Interface of the Stopwatch is shown in Figure 22.3

Figure 22.3

22.3 Creating a Digital Dice

We can create a digital dice easily using the Timer Control. To create a dice, you need to generate random numbers using the Rnd function. Rnd generates numbers between 0 and 1. The statement

$$n = Int(1 + Rnd() * 6)$$

generates integers from 1 to 6 randomly.

In the code, we introduce the variable m to control the length of time of the rolling process. If m is more than 1000, then the rolling process will stop by setting the timer enabled property to False.

The code is shown below:

```
Public Class Form1

Dim n, m As Integer

Private Sub Timer1_Tick(ByVal sender As System.Object, ByVal e As
System.EventArgs) Handles Timer1.Tick

        m = m + 10

        If m < 1000 Then

        n = Int(1 + Rnd() * 6)

        LblDice.Text = n

        Else

        Timer1.Enabled = False

        m = 0

        End If

End Sub

Private Sub RollDiceBtn_Click(ByVal sender As System.Object, ByVal e As
System.EventArgs) Handles RollDiceBtn.Click

        Timer1.Enabled = True

End Sub
```

Running the program produces a dice with fast changing numbers , which stop at a certain number. The interface is shown in Figure22.4

Figure 22.4: Animated Dice

Summary

In this chapter, you learned how to use Timer to create various applications.

➤ In section 22.1, you learned how to create a clock.

➤ In section 22.2, you learned how to create a stopwatch.

➤ In section 22.3, you learned how to create a digital dice.

Chapter 23

Creating Animation

❖ Learning how to create Animation in VB2010

Although VB2010 is a serious programming language designed for creating business and other industrial applications and not for creating animation, you can use it to create animation and other fun programs. In this Chapter, we will show you just that.

23.1 Moving an object

In this section, we will show you how to move an object by pressing a command button. You need to make use of the **Top** and **Left** properties of an object to create animation. The Top property defines the distance of the object from the top most border of the screen while the Left property defines the distance of the object from leftmost border of the screen. By adding or subtracting the distance of the object, we can create the animated effect of moving an object.

Start a new project and name it as Movable Object, or any name you wish. Now insert a Picture Box and in its Image property import a picture from your hard drive or other sources. Next, insert four command buttons and set their properties as in Table 23.1.

Control	Property
Button1	Name: MoveUpBtn Text : Move Up
Button2	Name: MoveDownBtn Text : Move Down
Button3	Name: MoveLeftBtn Text : Move Left
Button4	Name: MoveRightBtn Text : Move Right

Table 23.1

Now, click on the buttons and key in the following code:

```
Private Sub MoveDownBtn_Click(ByVal sender As System.Object, ByVal e As
System.EventArgs) Handles MoveDownBtn.Click

        PictureBox1.Top = PictureBox1.Top + 10

End Sub

Private Sub MoveLeftBtn_Click(ByVal sender As System.Object, ByVal e As
System.EventArgs) Handles MoveLeftBtn.Click

        PictureBox1.Left = PictureBox1.Left - 10

End Sub

Private Sub MoveRightBtn_Click(ByVal sender As System.Object, ByVal e As
System.EventArgs) Handles MoveRightBtn.Click

        PictureBox1.Left = PictureBox1.Left + 10

End Sub
```

Explanation:

Each time the user clicks on the Move Down button, the distance of the PictureBox increases by 10 pixels from the top border, creating a downward motion. On the other hand, each time the user clicks on the Move Up button, the distance of the PictureBox decreases by 10 pixels from the top borders, thus creating an upward motion. In addition, each time the user click on the Move Left button, the distance of the PictureBox decreases by 10 pixels from the left border, thus creating a leftward motion. Lastly, each time the user click on the Move Right button, the distance of the PictureBox increases by 10 pixels from the left border, thus creating a rightward motion.

The interface is shown in Figure 23.1

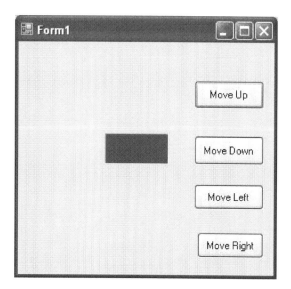

Figure 23.1

23.2 Creating Animation Using Timer

We can create continuous animation using timer without the need to manually clicking a command button. We can create left to right or top to bottom motion by writing the necessary code.

First, insert a PictureBox into the form. In the PictureBox properties window, select the image property and click to import an image file from your external sources such as your hard drive, your Pendrive or DVD. We have inserted an image of a bunch of grapes. Next, insert a Timer control into the form set its interval property to 100, which is equivalent to 0.1 second. We also set its Enabled property to be false so that the animation will not start when the form is loaded. Finally, add two command buttons to the form, name one of them as AnimateBtn and the other one as StopBtn, and change to caption to Animate and Stop respectively.

We make use of the Left property of the PictureBox to create the motion. PictureBox.Left means the distance of the PictureBox from the left border of the Form. Now click on the Timer control and type in the following code:

```
Private Sub Timer1_Tick(ByVal sender As System.Object, ByVal e As
System.EventArgs) Handles Timer1.Tick
        If PictureBox1.Left < Me.Width Then
        PictureBox1.Left = 0
        End PictureBox1.Left = PictureBox1.Left + 10
        Else
        If
End Sub
```

In the code above, Me.Width represents the width of the Form. If the distance of the PictureBox from the left is less than the width of the Form, a value of 10 is added to the distance of the PictureBox from the left border each time the Timer tick, or every 0.1 second in this example. When the distance of the PictureBox from the left border is equal to the width of the form, the distance from the left border is set to 0, which move the PictureBox object to the left border and then move right again, thus creates an oscillating motion from left to right. We need to insert a button to stop the motion. The code for the Stop button is:

```
        Timer1.Enabled = False
```

To animate the PictureBox object, we click the Animate button and key in the following code:

```
        Timer1.Enabled = True
```

The Interface of the Animation program is show in Figure 23.2

When the user click on the Animate button, the image will move from left to right continuously until the user press the Stop button.

Figure 23.2

23.3 Creating a Simple Lucky Seven Slot Machine

A lucky seven slot machine allows a player to win the jackpot if three rows of 7 appear when the spin stopped. In this example, we can create a simple version of the lucky seven slot machine with only one row of numbers. In this program, we insert three labels, a button and a timer into the form. Set the properties of the controls as follows:

Control	Property
Label1, Label2 and Label3	Backcolor: Navy Blue
	Forecolor: Yellow
	Font: Microsoft Sans Serif, Size 14, Bold
Button1	Name : BtnSpin Text : SPIN
	Font: Microsoft Sans Serif, Size 14, Bold
Button1	Name : BtnSpin Text : EXIT
	Font: Microsoft Sans Serif, Size 14, Bold

Table 23.2

We need to write code that generates nine numbers that changes randomly according to the Timer's interval and displays them on the three labels. The process stops after a certain period. The program will then examine the final three numbers. If the three numbers are found to be seven, a message will pop up to tell the player that he has won the jackpot, otherwise the message will display the text " No luck, try again".

To generate random numbers, we use the Rnd() function. The syntax to generate nine integers from 1 to 9 is shown below:

$$Int(1 + Rnd(\ ) * 9)$$

You need to declare three variables n1, n2, and n3 as integers so that the randomly generated numbers will be assigned to them and to be displayed on three labels. We also declare a variable m to control the duration of the spin. The value of m increases by 10 after each timer's interval and the process stops after the value of m exceeds 1000. Enter the code as shown below:

```
Public Class Form1
    Dim m, n1, n2, n3 As Integer

    Private Sub Form1_Load(ByVal sender As System.Object, ByVal e As
    System.EventArgs) Handles MyBase.Load

    End Sub

    Private Sub Timer1_Tick(ByVal sender As System.Object, ByVal e As
    System.EventArgs) Handles Timer1.Tick
        m = m + 10
        If m < 1000 Then
            n1 = Int(1 + Rnd() * 9)
            Label1.Text = n1
            n2 = Int(1 + Rnd() * 9)
            Label2.Text = n2
            n3 = Int(1 + Rnd() * 9)
            Label3.Text = n3
        Else
```

```
        Timer1.Enabled = False
        m = 0
        If n1 = 7 And n2 = 7 And n3 = 7 Then
            MsgBox("You strike Jackpot and won $1,000,000")
        Else
            MsgBox("No luck, try again")

        End If
    End If

    End Sub


Private Sub BtnSpin_Click(ByVal sender As System.Object, ByVal e As
System.EventArgs) Handles BtnSpin.Click
        Timer1.Enabled = True
    End Sub


Private Sub BtnExit_Click(ByVal sender As System.Object, ByVal e As
System.EventArgs) Handles BtnExit.Click
        End
    End Sub
End Class
```

The runtime interface is shown in Figure 23.3

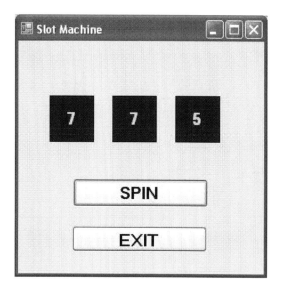

Figure 23.3

23.4 Creating a Graphical Slot Machine

We will modify the previous slot machine make it into a graphical one. Instead of displaying random numbers, this slot machine shows random images. To show the images randomly, we use the same logic as the previous example, but instead of generating random numbers, the program loads images randomly. The syntax to load image is:

```
Image.FromFile("C:\ My Documents\Image\image. jpg")
```

In this example, we insert three picture boxes for loading three different images. This program is for demonstration only so we use only three images so that the code does not look too complicated. We use the Select Case...End Select control structure to load images according to the values of the randomly generated numbers. The procedure to load the images randomly is:

```
n1 = Int(1 + Rnd( )* 3)

n2 = Int(1 + Rnd( )* 3)

n3 = Int(1 + Rnd( )* 3)

    Select Case n1
    Case 1
    PictureBox1.Image = Image.FromFile("C:\ MyDuments\Image\image1. jpg")
    Case 2
    PictureBox2.Image = Image.FromFile("C:\ MyDuments\Image\image2. jpg")
    Case 3
    PictureBox3.Image = Image.FromFile("C:\ MyDuments\Image\image3 jpg")

    End Select
```

We need to insert a timer to create the animation effect. In the properties window, set the property enabled to be false

The full code looks like this:

```
Public Class Form1

 Dim m, n1, n2, n3 As Integer


Private Sub Timer1_Tick(ByVal sender As System.Object, ByVal e As
System.EventArgs) Handles Timer1.Tick

 m = m + 10
 If m < 1000 Then

    n1 = Int(1 + Rnd() * 3)

    n2 = Int(1 + Rnd() * 3)

    n3 = Int(1 + Rnd() * 3)

    Select Case n1

      Case 1
      PictureBox1.Image = Image.FromFile("C:\ MyDuments\Image\image1. jpg")
      Case 2
      PictureBox1.Image = Image.FromFile("C:\ MyDuments\Image\image2. jpg")
      Case 3
       PictureBox1.Image = Image.FromFile("C:\ MyDuments\Image\image3. jpg")

    End Select

      Select Case n2

      Case 1
      PictureBox2.Image = Image.FromFile("C:\ MyDuments\Image\image1. jpg")
      Case 2
      PictureBox2.Image = Image.FromFile("C:\ MyDuments\Image\image2. jpg")
      Case 3
       PictureBox3.Image = Image.FromFile("C:\ MyDuments\Image\image3. jpg")

    End Select
```

```
        Select Case n3

         Case 1
         PictureBox3.Image = Image.FromFile("C:\ MyDuments\Image\image1. jpg")
         Case 2
         PictureBox3.Image = Image.FromFile("C:\ MyDuments\Image\image2. jpg")
         Case 3
         PictureBox3.Image = Image.FromFile("C:\ MyDuments\Image\image3. jpg")

        End Select


        Else
           Timer1.Enabled = False
           m = 0
           If n1 = n2 And n1 = n3 Then

              Label1.Text = "Jackpot! You won $1,000,000"
           Else
              Label1.Text = "No luck, try again"

           End If

        End If
    End Sub
    Private Sub BtnSpin_Click(ByVal sender As System.Object, ByVal e As
    System.EventArgs) Handles BtnSpin.Click
        Label1.Text = ""
        Timer1.Enabled = True
    End Sub
    Private Sub BtnExit_Click(ByVal sender As System.Object, ByVal e As
    System.EventArgs) Handles BtnExit.Click
        End
```

End Sub

End Class

The interface is shown in Figure 23.4

Figure 23.4

Summary

In this chapter, you learned how to create animation.

> ➤ In section 23.1, you learned how to write code that move an object.

> ➤ In section 23.2, you learned how to use Timer to create animation.

> ➤ In section 23.3, you learned how to create a lucky seven slot machine.

> ➤ In section 23.4, you learned how to create a graphical slot machine.

Chapter 24

Adding Menus and Toolbar

❖ Learning how to Create Menus and Menu Items

❖ Learning how to Create Toolbar Items

Menus and toolbars remain as the standard features of all windows applications despite the development of more sophisticated GUI. The menu bar contains menus, which contain groups of menu items that the user can used to execute certain commands to perform certain tasks like opening a file, saving a file, printing a page, formatting a page and more. On the other hand, a standard toolbar displays icons that can be used to open a file, save a file, viewing a document, printing a document and more.

In this chapter, we will show you how to add Menus and icons to the toolbar of your applications. We will use the text editor from the chapter 19 but now we shall execute the commands using the menus and the toolbar icons. We shall also make this program more powerful by enabling it to format the text as well as to print out the text from the text file.

In this project, we will add MenuStrip1, ToolStrip1, SaveFileDialog1, OpenFileDialog1,PrintDialog1 and FontDialog1 controls to the form.

24.1 Adding Menus

Open the text editor file from the chapter 19, but now we will clear the buttons and add menus instead. First, drag the Menu Strip and position it at the top part of the form. Add the first top-level menu by typing it in the textbox that appears with a blurred text "Type Here". The first menu you will add is File, but you type it with the ampersand sign in front, like this, &File. The reason is the ampersand sign will underline the letter F, File at runtime so that the user can use the keyboard short-cut keys to execute a command. The second top-level menu that we shall add is Format, which we type it as &Format.

The next step is to add menu items to the File and the Format Menu. The three menu items that we are going to add to the File menu are Open, Save, Print and Exit, type them as &Open, &Save, &Print and E&xit. The menu items that we will add to the Format menu are Font (type it as Fo&nt), Font Color (type it as Font &Color) and Background Color (type it as &Background Color). The menu items can be moved upward or downward easily by dragging them. They can be deleted easily by pressing the right mouse button and then click deleted in the pop-up dialog.

When we run the finished design, we shall see a window application that comprises menus and menu items, as shown in Figure 241. Notice the underlined characters of the menu items.

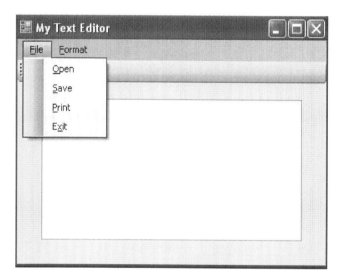

Figure 24.1

24.1.1 Writing Code for the Menu Items

The application in the preceding section is not able to do anything yet until we write code for the menu items.

The menu item **Open** should execute a command that will allow the user to choose a file from a storage source and open it via a pop-up dialog. The code is the same as the code to read text file in the previous chapter. It involves the use of the OpenFileDialog control. Now, double click on the Open menu item and enter the code as follows:

```
Private Sub OpenToolStripMenuItem_Click(ByVal sender As System.Object, ByVal e
As System.EventArgs) Handles OpenToolStripMenuItem.Click
    Dim FileReader As StreamReader
    Dim results As DialogResult
    results = OpenFileDialog1.ShowDialog
    If results = DialogResult.OK Then
        FileReader = New StreamReader(OpenFileDialog1.FileName)
        TxtEditor.Text = FileReader.ReadToEnd( )
        FileReader.Close( )
    End If
  End Sub
```

Remember place the statement **Imports System.IO** before Public Class Form1 so that the program is able to read the file. The open dialog is shown in Figure 24.2

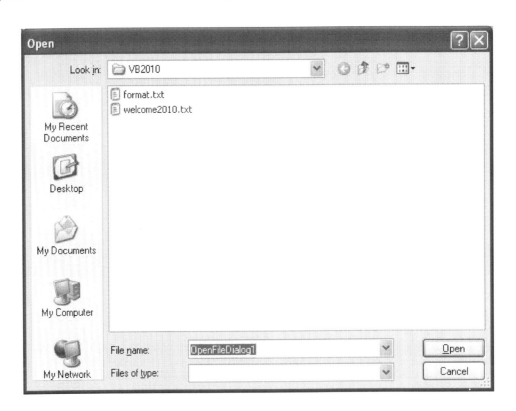

Figure 24.2

Menu item **Save** executes command that writes file to the computer storage unit. The code is the same as the code for writing file in the previous chapter. Click on the Save menu item and enter the following code:

```
Private Sub SaveToolStripMenuItem_Click(ByVal sender As System.Object, ByVal e As System.EventArgs) Handles SaveToolStripMenuItem.Click
    Dim FileWriter As StreamWriter
    Dim results As DialogResult
    results = SaveFileDialog1.ShowDialog
    If results = DialogResult.OK Then
        FileWriter = New StreamWriter(SaveFileDialog1.FileName, False)
        FileWriter.Write(TxtEditor.Text)
        FileWriter.Close()
    End If
End Sub
```

Writing code for the Print command requires the use of the PrintDialog control. It comprises two parts, the first part is to presents a print dialog for the user to set the options to print and second part is to print the document. Click on the print menu item and enter the following code:

i) The code to presents a print dialog

```
Private Sub PrintToolStripMenuItem_Click(ByVal sender As System.Object, ByVal e As System.EventArgs) Handles PrintToolStripMenuItem.Click
    'Let the user to choose the page range to print.
    PrintDialog1.AllowSomePages = True
    'Display the help button.
    PrintDialog1.ShowHelp = True
```

```vb
    PrintDialog1.Document = docToPrint


    Dim result As DialogResult = PrintDialog1.ShowDialog()
    If (result = DialogResult.OK) Then
        docToPrint.Print()
    End If


End Sub
```

ii) The code to print the document

```vb
Private Sub document_PrintPage(ByVal sender As Object, _
    ByVal e As System.Drawing.Printing.PrintPageEventArgs) _
        Handles docToPrint.PrintPage
    Dim mytext As String
    mytext = TxtEditor.Text
    Dim printFont As New System.Drawing.Font _
        ("Arial", 12, System.Drawing.FontStyle.Regular)

    ' Format and print the text
    e.Graphics.DrawString(mytext, printFont, _
        System.Drawing.Brushes.Black, 10, 10)
End Sub
```

24.2 Adding Toolbar Icons

Still using the same file, we shall now add some toolbar items in form of icons. You can lookup for some free icons sites in Google to download the icons you intend to place on your toolbar. In our example, we need six icons namely the Open icon, the Save icon, the Print icon, the Font Style and Formatting icon, the Font Color icon and the Background Color icon.

To add items to the toolbar, click on the small icon on the leftmost corner of the toolbar and choose button from the dropdown list, as shown in Figure 25.3

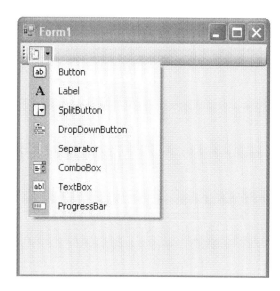

Figure 24.3

Right click on the button and choose properties window from the dropdown list, then proceed to change the default image by clicking the three-dot button on the right of the image property. Choose an icon or image file from your hard drive that you wish to load, as shown in Figure 24.4 and Figure 24.5

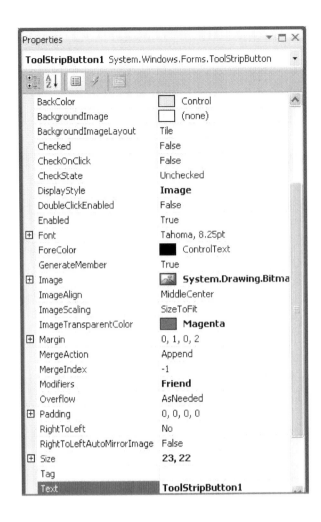

Figure 25.4: Properties window of the ToolStrp Button

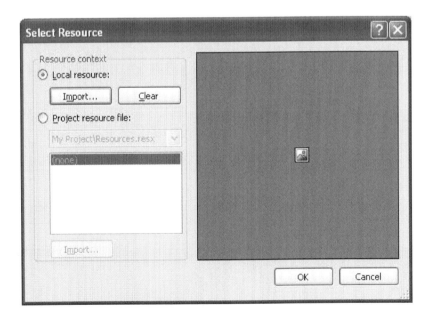

Figure 24.5: Dialog to select image file

Using the aforementioned method, we have added the following toolbar items and set their properties as shown in Table 24.1. The ToolTipText is to display text when the user places his or her mouse over the toolbar icon. The purpose is to provide information about the action that can be executed by clicking the icon.

Toolbar Item	Name	ToolTipText
	ToolOpen	Open
	ToolSave	Save
	ToolPrint	Print
	ToolFontStyle	Font Style and Formatting
	ToolFontColor	Font Color
	ToolBkColor	Background Color

The finished interface is shown in Figure 24.6

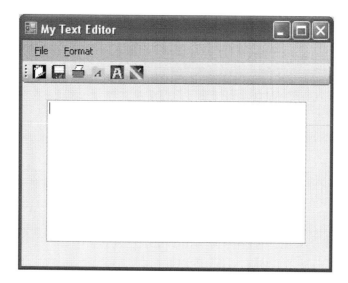

Figure 24.6

Next, we shall write code for every item on the tool bar. The codes are the same as the codes we programmed for the menu items.

Open Folder	

The Code:

```
Private Sub ToolOpen_Click(ByVal sender As System.Object, ByVal e As
System.EventArgs) Handles ToolOpen.Click
    Dim FileReader As StreamReader
    Dim results As DialogResult
    results = OpenFileDialog1.ShowDialog
    If results = DialogResult.OK Then
        FileReader = New StreamReader(OpenFileDialog1.FileName)
        TxtEditor.Text = FileReader.ReadToEnd()
        FileReader.Close()
    End If
End Sub
```

Save File	

The Code:

```
Private Sub ToolSave_Click(ByVal sender As System.Object, ByVal e As
System.EventArgs) Handles ToolSave.Click
    Dim FileWriter As StreamWriter
    Dim results As DialogResult
    results = SaveFileDialog1.ShowDialog
    If results = DialogResult.OK Then
        FileWriter = New StreamWriter(SaveFileDialog1.FileName, False)
```

```
        FileWriter.Write(TxtEditor.Text)

        FileWriter.Close()

    End If

End Sub
```

Print	

The Code

```
Private Sub ToolPrint_Click(ByVal sender As System.Object, ByVal e As
System.EventArgs) Handles ToolPrint.Click

    PrintDialog1.AllowSomePages = True

    PrintDialog1.ShowHelp = True

    PrintDialog1.Document = docToPrint

    Dim result As DialogResult = PrintDialog1.ShowDialog()

    If (result = DialogResult.OK) Then
        docToPrint.Print()
    End If


End Sub
```

Format Font Style	

The Code

```
Private Sub ToolFontStyle_Click(ByVal sender As System.Object, ByVal e As
System.EventArgs) Handles ToolFontStyle.Click
    FontDialog1.ShowColor = True

    FontDialog1.Font = TxtEditor.Font

    FontDialog1.Color = TxtEditor.ForeColor
```

```
    If FontDialog1.ShowDialog() <> DialogResult.Cancel Then

        TxtEditor.Font = FontDialog1.Font

        TxtEditor.ForeColor = FontDialog1.Color

    End If

  End Sub
```

Font Color	

The Code

```
 Private Sub ToolFontColor_Click(ByVal sender As System.Object, ByVal e As
System.EventArgs) Handles ToolFontColor.Click

    Dim MyDialog As New ColorDialog()

    MyDialog.AllowFullOpen = False

    MyDialog.ShowHelp = True

    MyDialog.Color = TxtEditor.ForeColor

    If (MyDialog.ShowDialog() = Windows.Forms.DialogResult.OK) Then

        TxtEditor.ForeColor = MyDialog.Color

    End If

 End Sub
```

Background Color	

The Code

```
Private Sub ToolBkColor_Click(ByVal sender As System.Object, ByVal e As
System.EventArgs) Handles ToolBkColor.Click

    Dim MyDialog As New ColorDialog()
```

```
    MyDialog.AllowFullOpen = False

    MyDialog.ShowHelp = True

    MyDialog.Color = TxtEditor.BackColor

     If (MyDialog.ShowDialog() = Windows.Forms.DialogResult.OK) Then

       TxtEditor.BackColor = MyDialog.Color

    End If

  End Sub
```

To test the program, press F5 to run it. Enter the Text "Welcome to Visual Basic 2010 programming" into the text editor, then use the menu items or the toolbar icons to change the font size to 14 ,font color to yellow and the background color to blue. You will see the menus and toolbar icons appear on top of the text editor, as shown in Figure 24.7

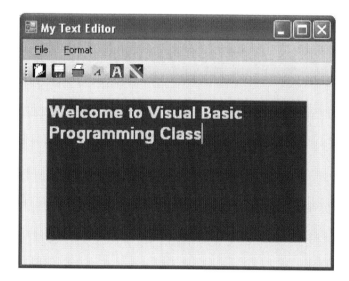

Figure 24.7

Summary

In this chapter, you learned how to add menus and toolbar to your application.

 ➢ In section 24.1, you learned how to add menus to your application, a text editor. You also learned how to write code for the menus. Besides, you learned to write code for printing the text.

 ➢ In section 24.2, you learned how to add toolbar icons and write code for them.

Chapter 25

Packaging Applications for Distribution

❖ Learning how to use publish wizard to package applications for distribution

---

By now, you have learned how to create many useful applications in VB2010, It is time for you to distribute them to your friends or even sell them to your potential customers. However, it is not possible to distribute your applications in the raw code form; you need to package them into a distributable form before you can deploy them. To package your application means you need to create an install program so that the user can install your application in his or her computer. You can choose to create an install program that the users can download from the web, or you can create an install program that you can distribute using CD ROM, DVD ROM, pen drive or external hard disk..

25.1 Creating the Setup Program using Publish Wizard

The application we will package here is the text editor we have created in Chapter 24. To start setting up the program, open the text editor project. Once loaded, click project on the menu and then choose publish TxtEditor. Click on publish TxtEditor and the Publish Wizard dialog appears, as shown in Figure 25.1

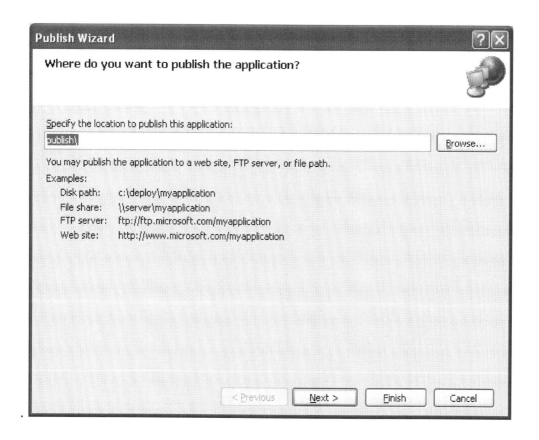

Figure 25.1: The Publish Wizard Dialog

In the Publish Wizard dialog, you need to enter a location to publish your application. You have the options to publish your application to a web site, FTP server or your local drive. We will only publish the application to a local drive. To create the install program in your local drive, you need to click browse and look for a folder in your hard drive where the files will be setup there. It is advisable to create a folder before you start publishing your application; here we have created the vb2010apps folder in My Documents. On my computer, the path is

C:\Documents and Settings\Voon Kiong Liew\My Documents\vb2010apps

Your path will be different form mine.

After choosing the path, the location will show up in the Publish Wizard as shown in Figure 25.2

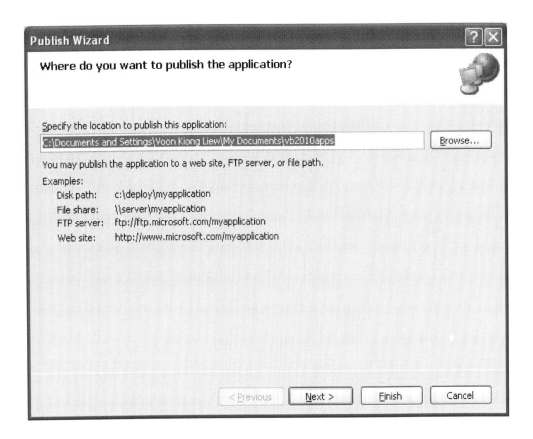

Figure 25.2

Now click the Next button and you can see another dialog asking you the options of how you want your users to install the application, as shown in Figure 25.3. We choose installation from CR_ROM or DVD_ROM.

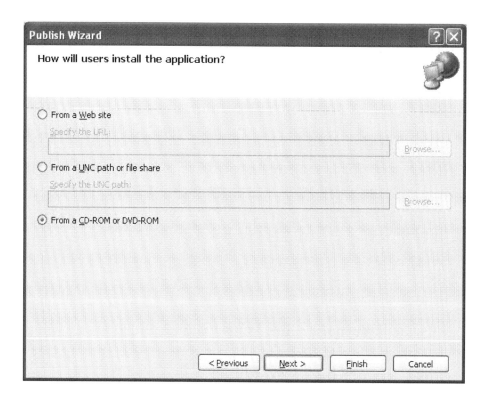

Figure 25.3: Mode of Installation

Click Next and you will see another dialog asking you where the application will check for updates, as shown in Figure 25.4. In our case, we choose not to check updates option.

Figure 25.4

The next dialog will remind you to check your application weather it is ready for deployment, as shown in Figure 25.5.

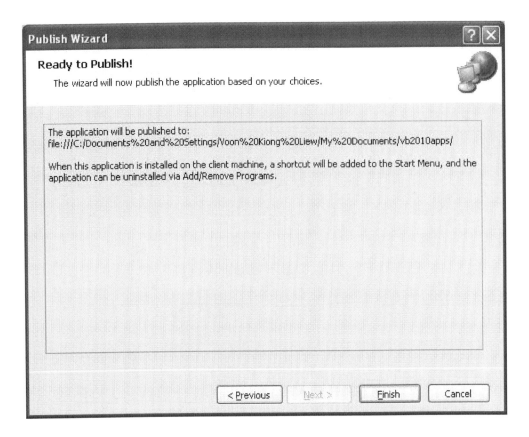

Figure 25.5

If you are certain that your application contains no errors then click finish. The Publish Wizard will start compiling your files and set up the install files. Finally, it will open the folder and display the install files, including the setup.exe file, as shown in Figure 25.6

Figure 25.6

25.2 Testing your Install Program

Now it is time to test out the install program for your TxtEditor. Click the setup.exe file to start the installation process. The first dialog that appears issues a security warning as your application was not licensed digitally. However, since you have created your own application and you are sure it will not cause any harm to your computer, simply click the install button to continue with the installation process. As soon as the installation completes, it will launch the installed application.

To look up for your newly installed application, you can click the start menu in your window and click on All Programs and you will be see the TxtEditor folder which contains the TxtEditor application where you can click to run the program, as shown in Figure 25.7. To distribute your application, simply copy the install folder and files to a CD-ROM, A DVD-ROM or a Pen Drive.

Figure 25.7

Summary

In this chapter, you learned how to package and distribution your application

➢ In section 25.1, you learned how to create the install program using the Publish Wizard.
➢ In section 25.2, you learned how to test your install program

Appendix I

The ASCII Table

#		#		#		#		#		#		#		#	
1	☺	31		61	=	91	[	121	y	151	—	181	µ	211	Ó
2	☻	32		62	>	92	\	122	z	152	˜	182	¶	212	Ô
3	♥	33	!	63	?	93	]	123	{	153	™	183	·	213	Õ
4	♦	34	"	64	@	94	^	124	|	154	š	184	¸	214	Ö
5	♣	35	#	65	A	95	_	125	}	155	›	185	¹	215	×
6	–	36	$	66	B	96	`	126	~	156	œ	186	º	216	Ø
7	•	37	%	67	C	97	A	127		157	▯	187	»	217	Ù
8	▫	38	&	68	D	98	B	128	€	158	ž	188	¼	218	Ú
9	♪	39	'	69	E	99	C	129	▯	159	Ÿ	189	½	219	Û
10		40	(	70	F	100	D	130	,	160		190	¾	220	Ü
11	♂	41	)	71	G	101	E	131	ƒ	161	¡	191	¿	221	Ý
12	♀	42	*	72	H	102	F	132	„	162	¢	192	À	222	Þ
13	♪	43	+	73	I	103	G	133	…	163	£	193	Á	223	ß
14	♫	44	,	74	J	104	H	134	†	164	¤	194	Â	224	à
15	☼	45	-	75	K	105	I	135	‡	165	¥	195	Ã	225	á
16	†	46	.	76	L	106	j	136	ˆ	166	¦	196	Ä	226	â
17	◄	47	/	77	M	107	k	137	‰	167	§	197	Å	227	ã
18	↕	48	0	78	N	108	l	138	Š	168	¨	198	Æ	228	ä
19	‼	49	1	79	O	109	m	139	‹	169	©	199	Ç	229	å
20	¶	50	2	80	P	110	n	140	Œ	170	ª	200	È	230	æ
21	⊥	51	3	81	Q	111	o	141	▯	171	«	201	É	231	ç
22	⊤	52	4	82	R	112	p	142	Ž	172	¬	202	Ê	232	è
23	⊣	53	5	83	S	113	q	143	▯	173		203	Ë	233	é
24	↑	54	6	84	T	114	r	144	▯	174	®	204	Ì	234	ê
25	⊢	55	7	85	U	115	s	145	'	175	¯	205	Í	235	ë
26	→	56	8	86	V	116	t	146	'	176	°	206	Î	236	ì
27	←	57	9	87	W	117	u	147	"	177	±	207	Ï	237	í
28		58	:	88	X	118	v	148	"	178	²	208	Ð	238	î
29		59	;	89	Y	119	w	149	•	179	³	209	Ñ	239	ï
30	-	60	<	90	Z	120	x	150	–	180	´	210	Ò	240	ð

#		#		#	
241	ñ				
242	ò				
243	ó				
244	ô				
245	õ				
246	ö				
247	÷				
248	ø				
249	ù				
250	ú				
251	û				
252	ü				
253	ý				
254	þ				
255	ÿ				

Appendix II

List of Culture Codes

Code	Language - Country/Region	Code	Language - Country/Region
af	Afrikaans	hu-HU	Hungarian - Hungary
af-ZA	Afrikaans - South Africa	is	Icelandic
sq	Albanian	is-IS	Icelandic - Iceland
sq-AL	Albanian – Albania	id	Indonesian
ar	Arabic	id-ID	Indonesian - Indonesia
ar-DZ	Arabic – Algeria	it	Italian
ar-BH	Arabic – Bahrain	it-IT	Italian - Italy
ar-EG	Arabic – Egypt	it-CH	Italian - Switzerland
ar-IQ	Arabic – Iraq	ia	Japanese
ar-JO	Arabic – Jordan	ia-JP	Japanese - Japan
ar-KW	Arabic – Kuwait	kn	Kannada
ar-LB	Arabic – Lebanon	kn-IN	Kannada - India
ar-LY	Arabic – Libya	kk	Kazakh
ar-MA	Arabic – Morocco	kk-KZ	Kazakh - Kazakhstan
ar-OM	Arabic – Oman	kok	Konkani
ar-QA	Arabic – Qatar	kok-IN	Konkani - India
ar-SA	Arabic - Saudi Arabia	ko	Korean
ar-SY	Arabic – Syria	ko-KR	Korean - Korea
ar-TN	Arabic – Tunisia	ky	Kyrgyz
ar-AE	Arabic - United Arab Emirates	ky-KG	Kyrgyz - Kyrgyzstan
ar-YE	Arabic – Yemen	lv	Latvian
hy	Armenian	lv-LV	Latvian - Latvia
hy-AM	Armenian – Armenia	lt	Lithuanian
az	Azeri	lt-LT	Lithuanian - Lithuania
az-AZ-	Azeri (Cyrillic) – Azerbaijan	mk	Macedonian
az-AZ-	Azeri (Latin) – Azerbaijan	mk-MK	Macedonian - Former Yugoslav Republic
eu	Basque	ms	Malay
eu-ES	Basque – Basque	ms-BN	Malay - Brunei

be	Belarusian	ms-MY	Malay - Malaysia
be-BY	Belarusian – Belarus	mr	Marathi
bg	Bulgarian	mr-IN	Marathi - India
bg-BG	Bulgarian – Bulgaria	mn	Mongolian
ca	Catalan	mn-MN	Mongolian - Mongolia
ca-ES	Catalan – Catalan	no	Norwegian
zh-HK	Chinese - Hong Kong SAR	nb-NO	Norwegian (Bokm?l) - Norway
zh-MO	Chinese - Macao SAR	nn-NO	Norwegian (Nynorsk) - Norway
zh-CN	Chinese – China	pl	Polish
zh-CHS	Chinese (Simplified)	pl-PL	Polish - Poland
zh-SG	Chinese – Singapore	pt	Portuguese
zh-TW	Chinese – Taiwan	pt-BR	Portuguese - Brazil
zh-CHT	Chinese (Traditional)	pt-PT	Portuguese - Portugal
hr	Croatian	pa	Punjabi
hr-HR	Croatian – Croatia	pa-IN	Punjabi - India
cs	Czech	ro	Romanian
cs-CZ	Czech - Czech Republic	ro-RO	Romanian - Romania
da	Danish	ru	Russian
da-DK	Danish – Denmark	ru-RU	Russian - Russia
div	Dhivehi	sa	Sanskrit
div-MV	Dhivehi – Maldives	sa-IN	Sanskrit - India
nl	Dutch	sr-SP-	Serbian (Cyrillic) - Serbia
nl-BE	Dutch – Belgium	sr-SP-	Serbian (Latin) - Serbia
nl-NL	Dutch - The Netherlands	sk	Slovak
en	English	sk-SK	Slovak - Slovakia
en-AU	English – Australia	sl	Slovenian
en-BZ	English – Belize	sl-SI	Slovenian - Slovenia
en-CA	English – Canada	es	Spanish
en-CB	English – Caribbean	es-AR	Spanish - Argentina
en-IE	English – Ireland	es-BO	Spanish - Bolivia
en-JM	English – Jamaica	es-CL	Spanish - Chile
en-NZ	English - New Zealand	es-CO	Spanish - Colombia
en-PH	English – Philippines	es-CR	Spanish - Costa Rica

en-ZA	English - South Africa	es-DO	Spanish - Dominican Republic
en-TT	English - Trinidad and Tobago	es-EC	Spanish - Ecuador
en-GB	English - United Kingdom	es-SV	Spanish - El Salvador
en-US	English - United States	es-GT	Spanish - Guatemala
en-ZW	English – Zimbabwe	es-HN	Spanish - Honduras
et	Estonian	es-MX	Spanish - Mexico
et-EE	Estonian – Estonia	es-NI	Spanish - Nicaragua
fo	Faroese	es-PA	Spanish - Panama
fo-FO	Faroese - Faroe Islands	es-PY	Spanish - Paraguay
fa	Farsi	es-PE	Spanish - Peru
fa-IR	Farsi – Iran	es-PR	Spanish - Puerto Rico
fi	Finnish	es-ES	Spanish - Spain
fi-FI	Finnish – Finland	es-UY	Spanish - Uruguay
fr	French	es-VE	Spanish - Venezuela
fr-BE	French – Belgium	sw	Swahili
fr-CA	French – Canada	sw-KE	Swahili - Kenya
fr-FR	French – France	sv	Swedish
fr-LU	French – Luxembourg	sv-FI	Swedish - Finland
fr-MC	French – Monaco	sv-SE	Swedish - Sweden
fr-CH	French – Switzerland	syr	Syriac
gl	Galician	syr-SY	Syriac - Syria
gl-ES	Galician – Galician	ta	Tamil
ka	Georgian	ta-IN	Tamil - India
ka-GE	Georgian – Georgia	tt	Tatar
de	German	tt-RU	Tatar - Russia
de-AT	German – Austria	te	Telugu
de-DE	German – Germany	te-IN	Telugu - India
de-LI	German – Liechtenstein	th	Thai
de-LU	German – Luxembourg	th-TH	Thai - Thailand
de-CH	German – Switzerland	tr	Turkish
el	Greek	tr-TR	Turkish - Turkey
el-GR	Greek – Greece	uk	Ukrainian
gu	Gujarati	uk-UA	Ukrainian - Ukraine

gu-IN	Gujarati – India	ur	Urdu
he	Hebrew	ur-PK	Urdu - Pakistan
he-IL	Hebrew – Israel	uz	Uzbek
hi	Hindi	uz-UZ-	Uzbek (Cyrillic) - Uzbekistan
hi-IN	Hindi – India	uz-UZ-	Uzbek (Latin) - Uzbekistan
hu	Hungarian	vi	Vietnamese

Index

Printed in Great Britain
by Amazon.co.uk, Ltd.,
Marston Gate.